# If You Are Retiring, You Might Join the Peace Corps!

**SALLY JO NELSON BOTZLER**

with Richard George Botzler, RPCVs

Peace Corps Mexico (2009–2011)

WESTBOW
P R E S S®
A DIVISION OF THOMAS NELSON
& ZONDERVAN

WestBow Press books may be ordered through booksellers or by contacting:

WestBow Press
A Division of Thomas Nelson & Zondervan
1663 Liberty Drive
Bloomington, IN 47403
www.westbowpress.com
1 (866) 928-1240

ISBN: 978-1-5127-9714-5 (sc)
ISBN: 978-1-5127-9715-2 (e)

Library of Congress Control Number: 2017911716

Print information available on the last page.

WestBow Press rev. date: 07/28/2017

This book is dedicated to the memory of Lillian Gordy Carter, whose example of post-retirement Peace Corps service is an inspiration!

# Contents

# *Preface*

Members of the baby-boomer generation are among a particularly large group of Americans who have approached the time of retirement with good health—physically, economically, and spiritually. Today's retirees are able to enjoy active lives, and many already have been volunteering for several years in service projects within their local communities, churches, synagogues, and mosques. Increasing numbers of US retirees are living full and independent lives. Many are seeking additional ways to contribute to the well-being of others. If you are retiring, you might consider international community service by joining the Peace Corps!

In December 2007, when we were in our midsixties, my husband Rick and I both retired from our positions as professors at Humboldt State University (HSU) in Arcata, California. Both of us had volunteered in community and church projects throughout our adult lives, and we had enjoyed international travel experiences with our family. Soon after our retirement, we applied to become volunteers in the US Peace Corps program. We felt fortunate to be selected as a couple to serve in Peace Corps Mexico (http://now.humboldt.edu/news/retired-faculty-join-peace-corps-ranks/).

During our twenty-seven months of volunteer service in Peace Corps Mexico, we regularly e-mailed updates to family and friends who had asked us to keep them informed about our experiences. This small book is a collection of those summaries, organized by date, and includes photos and online links that accompanied the updates. Some adjustments have been made to aid clarity. Later in the book, there are descriptions of several hidden benefits and challenges that Rick and I discovered—sometimes with considerable surprise.

As young adults, both of us had found the first announcements about the proposed US Peace Corps program exciting and inspiring. On October 14, 1960, when Senator John F. Kennedy was a candidate for the presidency of the United States, he gave a speech at the University of Michigan in Ann Arbor in which he shared the concept of international community service that ultimately became the Peace Corps (see http://peacecorps.umich.edu/Tobin.html).

This extemporaneous speech at U of M was reflected in the challenge that President Kennedy later enunciated in his inaugural address on January 20, 1961, in Washington, DC. He boldly proclaimed, "Ask not what your country can do for you—ask what you can do for your country" (https://www.jfklibrary.org/Asset-Viewer/BqXIEM9F4024ntFl7SVAjA.aspx).

Although President Kennedy's clarion call for international civilian service and the start of the Peace Corps program strongly resonated with Rick and me, at that time in the early 1960s, both of us were enrolled as students at Detroit's Wayne State University. The two of us were just beginning our postsecondary education, and we were committed college students.

Then, in November 1963, Rick and I married during my last year of college. At that time, my major was in the field of education, and Rick was beginning his graduate studies in biological sciences at Wayne. In spring 1964, we moved from Detroit to Ann Arbor so that Rick could continue his graduate studies. Happily, I was hired for my first year of teaching in nearby Plymouth, Michigan. By summer 1965, I was pregnant with our first baby, and Emi was born in April 1966. At this same time, US involvement in the war in Vietnam was intensifying.

Until this time, Rick had been granted educational deferments by the US draft board. In spring 1966, educational deferments were no longer valid, and American men were eligible for deferments only if they had families with children. A letter from our family doctor in Ann Arbor documented Rick's fatherhood and allowed him to have his deferment continued.

Thus it was that our thoughts of Peace Corps service were postponed. Yet the possibility of international community service remained in our hearts and minds even after we relocated to Northern California for Rick's first professional position in 1970. Over the next four decades, Rick and I focused our energies on developing our careers and raising our five children.

Soon after we retired from HSU in December 2007, we applied for Peace Corps service as a couple. The application process required personal statements about our motivations, descriptions of our previous cross-cultural experiences, documentation that we were in good health physically and psychologically, résumés, recommendations, and financial disclosures. My responses to two of these requirements are included in Appendix A.

A returned volunteer who served as the Peace Corps recruiter at Humboldt State fielded our questions and provided a clear notion of what the program involved. Megan McDrew had been a student in one of my HSU graduate classes, and she helped us connect with other returned Peace Corps volunteers in our Northern California community; they shared experiences with us and addressed our concerns.

Rick and I soon learned that the mission of the Peace Corps includes three distinctive goals. As clearly stated on its website, "changing lives the world over, the Peace Corps is a service opportunity for motivated changemakers to immerse themselves in a community abroad, working side by side with local leaders to tackle the most pressing challenges of our generation." (See https://www.peacecorps.gov/about/.) The Peace Corps' mission is "to promote world peace and friendship by fulfilling three goals":

1. To help the people of interested countries in meeting their need for trained men and women.
2. To help promote a better understanding of Americans on the part of the peoples served.
3. To help promote a better understanding of other peoples on the part of Americans.

It was a great privilege for Rick and me to be accepted for Peace Corps service in Mexico. Our regular updates describe our experiences and the ways in which we did our best to fulfill the three goals. We truly cherish the friendships we made in Mexico, and we have endeavored to continue our connections with the people with whom we had the opportunity to work and learn.

Based on our positive experiences, we enthusiastically recommend Peace Corps service to others. We especially encourage the large numbers of retiring baby boomers in the United States to consider Peace Corps service among the variety of post-retirement options for community service. International Peace Corps service was life-changing for us, and we think others might find it challenging and beneficial too.

# Update 1

## March 1, 2009
## Peace Corps Mexico, Here We Come …

Hola from Rick and Sally! We are sending this message to you because you are on our e-mail LISTSERV for periodic updates about our Peace Corps Mexico experience. We plan to send two or three paragraphs and a photo or two every couple of weeks. If you would rather not receive this regular e-mail, please let us know right away, and we will take your address off the list. We understand completely that not everyone prefers to get news this way, so *do not hesitate* to tell us if you'd like your address removed.

The two of us will be flying to Washington, DC, tomorrow morning to meet the other fourteen Peace Corps Mexico volunteers with whom we will be involved in preservice preparations. Peace Corps staff in DC will provide one full day of orientation before our group flies to Mexico City and then takes a chartered bus up to Querétaro, where the Peace Corps Mexico headquarters is located. We'll be there for approximately twelve weeks of preservice preparation, which will include intensive Spanish-language and cultural-immersion activities. Once the preservice is successfully completed, our group of volunteers will be sworn in and assigned to our specific service regions and tasks. We'll keep you informed as the experience unfolds.

You might enjoy the brief news article that Humboldt State University published as an online news item: http://now.humboldt.edu/news/retired-faculty-join-peace-corps-ranks/. We were honored to be asked by the Peace Corps regional office for the San Francisco Bay Area to accept the Humboldt County Board of Supervisors' Proclamation for Peace Corps Week, which was February 23–March 1. Also, we enjoyed representing the Peace Corps last Thursday evening at the annual cultural fair at Morris School, the Spanish-immersion elementary school here in McKinleyville, where our grandchildren Olivia (first grade) and Nate (kindergarten) are enrolled. The event was well attended, and it was obvious that many of the children and their families are very interested in the Peace Corps history and mission.

We are filled with gratitude for this extraordinary opportunity to live and work with colleagues in Mexico for the next two years. We have so much to learn, and we look forward to this adventure with open minds and hearts.

Please keep in touch!
Warmly,
Rick and Sally

# Update 2

## March 15, 2009
## We've Received Our Peace Corps Mexico Assignments

This past Tuesday, March 10, the Peace Corps Mexico staff shared the volunteers' assignments for our two years of service. We will be going to the beautiful Sierra Gorda Biosphere Reserve in late May (following the completion of our preservice program) and will be living in Jalpan, which is located a few hours by car northeast of the city of Querétaro here in the state of the same name.

Rick and Sally in Mexico.

You can learn more about the reserve and its exact location at Earth Island Institute's interesting Viva Sierra Gorda website: http://www.earthisland.org/vivaSierraGorda/. We are thrilled to be able to live and work in this location. An orientation trip to Jalpan is scheduled for us sometime in April.

Our primary project assignments will build on the work of previous PC volunteers. Rick's initial assignment will involve monitoring of wildlife, including a jaguar population in the area. (He's not sure what proportion is actual fieldwork.) He also will be continuing some of the work in sales and certification within the carbon offset program that is being conducted on the reserve. Also, he probably will be doing some translation and editing of associated reports and publications.

Sally will be collaborating with reserve staff on a variety of education-related projects. For example, she will be working with guides in the reserve's ecotourism program to develop curricula and related materials for both face-to-face and virtual presentations for the many national and international tourists who visit each year. Also, she will assist the guides in developing stronger English skills for communicating with English-speaking tourists.

Attached is a group photo of us with our Peace Corps volunteer cohort taken on our day of arrival at the Peace Corps Mexico headquarters here in Querétaro. The staff and the facility are fabulous. The preservice program is very intense, and our Spanish is improving daily. It has been enjoyable to become acquainted with this remarkable group of staff and volunteers.

Peace Corps Mexico staff and volunteers.

We hope you are all doing well. We'll send another update in a couple of weeks!

Warmest greetings to you all,
Rick and Sally

# *Update 3*

## March 29, 2009
## Recent Visits to Other Peace Corps Mexico Volunteers

¡Hola, familia y amigos!

During the last few days, we have been visiting other Peace Corps volunteers serving in some of the more remote regions near Guadalajara in the state of Jalisco and in Ciudad Valles in the state of San Luis Potosí. The bus trips were long but well worth the travel time to observe more experienced volunteers in action.

Many of the Peace Corps Mexico projects involve an emphasis on environmental preservation, conservation, and education. Volunteers working on these kinds of projects collaborate with professional staff in SEMARNAT, a federal agency that has state and regional offices throughout Mexico. SEMARNAT actively promotes strategies such as ecotourism that have good potential for creating sustainable development in the country.

If you haven't already done so, we encourage you to check out the link to the Viva Sierra Gorda website that we sent in our last update. Again, you can read about this amazing place at http://www.earthisland.org/vivaSierraGorda/.

We will be visiting Jalpan and the Sierra Gorda in April for our first glimpse of the grandeur of our future home site. We look forward to moving to Jalpan sometime shortly after our Peace Corps swearing-in ceremony on May 22.

Peace Corps Mexico swearing-in ceremony.

Ángel Piñeda, Sally, Benita Luna, and Rick.

It's hard for us to believe that a third of our twelve-week preservice program here in Querétaro is completed. We are grateful to the excellent staff and Spanish-language teachers here in the Peace Corps Mexico office for doing their best to help us be prepared for the coming two years of service.

We'd love to hear news from all of you. Please keep in touch!

Con cariño,
Rick and Sally

# *Update 4*

## April 13, 2009
## Introducing Our Wonderful Host Family

¡Hola, familia y amigos!

For our Peace Corps Mexico update this time, we take great pleasure in introducing you to our host family here in Querétaro. Guadalupe and Antonio have three adult children, one teenage son, and six beautiful grandchildren. It has been a joy to become acquainted with the family!

Each PC volunteer here is required to complete a minimum of seventeen cultural activities in and around the Querétaro community during the preservice program. Lupe and Antonio have been more than generous in helping us fulfill this requirement. Recently, they guided us in a cooking activity in which Rick and I joined them in making a favorite family soup that originated in the Yucatan. Made with a variety of seafoods and fresh vegetables, including several kinds of chilies, the soup was delicious!

It has been very special for us to meet the six grandchildren. The kids adore Lupe and Antonio, and it warms our hearts to see the affection everyone in the family shares with one another. Lupe and Antonio enjoy African American jazz, soul, and blues, and they have several CDs they play regularly. Family events often end with the grandchildren dancing, and it's a delight to see!

Of course, our host family has helped us improve our Spanish too! Both Lupe and Antonio take great interest in history, and they have expanded our knowledge of Mexican history considerably by conversing with us as much as possible. ¡Muy bien!

The museums here in Querétaro are a rich source of regional and national history, archeology, and anthropology. Art institutes, theaters, and libraries abound as well. The city is known for the richness of its cultural heritage, and—as Lupe and Antonio have emphasized to us—the city and state will be an important part of the coming 2010 bicentennial celebration of Mexico's independence. We feel very fortunate to be living with Lupe and Antonio during the preservice period.

On Sunday, April 19, we will be heading to Jalpan in the Sierra Gorda Biosphere Reserve for a few days for our first site visit. We'll meet key leaders in the reserve, take a guided tour, and have a chance to look around Jalpan for an apartment or house. We are very excited about this initial visit to the place we'll be calling home for the next two years! This evening, we will be attending the Easter Sunday mass with Lupe and Antonio and their family.

We hope that all of you will enjoy a very happy Easter too!

Con cariño,
Rick and Sally

# *Update 5*

## April 26, 2009
## The Beautiful Sierra Gorda Biosphere Reserve

¡Hola, familia y amigos!

This past week, we spent three days at the Sierra Gorda Biosphere Reserve and the city of Jalpan as part of the Peace Corps Mexico future site visit program. We met the Sierra Gorda director, Martha (Pati) Ruíz Corzo (a former music teacher), as well as many other leaders and staff working in the reserve's various programs. They provided excellent orientations to their accomplishments, challenges, and goals. We feel fortunate to be assigned as Peace Corps volunteers (PCVs) to this pristine location! You might want to visit the dynamic, interactive Spanish-language Sierra Gorda website at http://sierragorda.net/.

We also had the good fortune to participate in two social events with members of the Sierra Gorda community as they bade farewell to two volunteers from a Japanese organization similar to the Peace Corps. We appreciated the hospitality of current PCVs Ben and Buffy Lenth, with whom we stayed in Jalpan. They are returning to the United States in mid-May. It seems likely that we will be able to rent the house where the Lenths have been living in the central district of Jalpan. It is just a twenty-minute walk to the reserve offices, where we will work along with fellow PCV Avram Primack.

We were inspired by the genuine love for the environment as well as the passion and vision of the Sierra Gorda leaders, staff, and community in working toward sustainable development. Both of us look forward to making connections in the community, improving our Spanish-language skills, and getting started with our projects—after we are sworn in on May 22 and have moved from Querétaro to Jalpan that weekend.

The Sierra Gorda directors and staff include several members of the Ruíz-Corzo extended family, which has occupied the region for six generations. They are dedicated to their work to restore, protect, and sustain this precious environment. The family's efforts over the years to work closely with the people living in the reserve areas have generated strong community relations and support. The directors and staff are inspired by the environment and seek to inspire others with their positive emotional attachment to the land. For example, Pati often has used music and song to capture the interest, enthusiasm, and commitment of people of all ages. (At our request, she sang a few favorite songs!)

Interestingly, use of Skype is routine among Sierra Gorda leaders and staff to maintain strong communication links. Communication is emphasized as a tool for success throughout the organization. We plan to participate in as many opportunities as possible, such as joining staff when they go out into the reserve environments during their workdays and signing up for some of the many workshops and online courses about the reserve and about environmental education. We enjoyed meeting a local artisan too. As you can imagine, we are eager to begin the next stage of this grand adventure!

As always, we'd love to hear news from all of you. Please keep in touch!

Con cariño,
Rick and Sally

# *Update 6 (To Family Only)*

## May 1, 2009
## Flu Epidemic

Dear ones:

As you know, there is a flu epidemic affecting several countries in the world, and it appears to have begun here in Mexico. The city (and state) of Querétaro where we are living during the preservice program has very few confirmed cases of the flu. We are feeling perfectly safe and well cared for by the Peace Corps leaders and staff.

Nonetheless, at the recommendation of Mexican president Felipe Calderon, the governor and the secretary for health in Querétaro announced the decision yesterday that most public offices, businesses, schools, and mass transportation systems were to be closed through next Wednesday, May 6. The schools have been closed since last Monday, and it remains to be seen whether they will reopen next Wednesday.

Yesterday afternoon, Peace Corps Mexico (PCM) country director Byron Battle announced that our preservice training program would be modified due to this national emergency. At the recommendation of the Peace Corps office in Washington, DC, Byron changed the status from "alert" to "standfast"—which means that volunteers and staff may not travel via mass transportation and that we need to remain in our locations and minimize outings in the communities. Therefore, we are working at our host family's home today, tomorrow, and Sunday. Monday and Tuesday, we will return to the PCM office for Spanish lessons during the mornings but will return to our homes in the afternoons.

Our host family has a computer, and we are able to hook up to the modem with our laptop. So we are still planning to Skype with as many of you as possible on Sunday afternoon. We are hoping to see you then.

How are *you*? Are there any flu cases in your communities? Have there been any school or business closures? We hope that you are all doing well and that you've not been exposed to this nasty virus. We've been advised here that the best preventative is frequent hand-washing since we humans are so prone to touching our faces. We have stepped up the routine and hope that you all are getting good advice for avoiding the flu in your areas. Let us know how things are going, okay?

Much love from Rick/Dad/Grandpa and Sally/Mom/Grandma

P.S. Today is May Day, which is the anniversary of the wedding of Great-Grandpa and Great-Grandma Stein (John and Johanna), who were married on May 1, 1889, in St. Clair, Michigan!

# Update 7

## May 9, 2009
## La Misma Luna

¡Hola, familia y amigos!

Hopefully, you will be enjoying the full moon tonight! Recently, the film *La Misma Luna* was shown in one of our Spanish classes. You may have seen the film in English. It documents with pathos the experiences of a young mother who feels compelled to leave her young son with her parents in Mexico while she tries to support him by working illegally in Los Angeles. This is a film worth seeing! Also, it is a comfort to know that when we are separated from our loved ones, we can look up into the beautiful night sky and behold the same moon—*la misma luna*.

As you are no doubt well aware, there has been a flu epidemic affecting several countries in the world, and it may have begun here in Mexico. The city (and state) of Querétaro where we are living during the preservice program has had few confirmed cases of the flu. We have felt perfectly safe and well cared for by the Peace Corps leaders and staff.

At the recommendation of President Calderon, the governor, and the secretary for health in Querétaro, most public offices, businesses, schools, and mass transportation systems were closed for several days. The elementary schools are reopening on Monday, May 11, and kids here are really excited to be able to get back to school and see all their friends again.

Our Peace Corps Mexico country director, Byron Battle, modified our training program due to the influenza epidemic. At the recommendation of the Peace Corps office in Washington, DC, Byron changed the status from "alert" to "standfast"—which meant that the volunteers and staff members were not able to travel via mass transportation and that we needed to remain in our locations and minimize outings in the communities. Yesterday, our status was changed back to "alert," and we have more freedom of movement.

How are *you*? Have there been any flu cases in your communities? Have there been any school or business closures? We hope that you are all doing well and that you've not been exposed to this form of the flu. Please let us know how things are going for you.

In less than two weeks, on Friday, May 22, we will be participating in the Peace Corps Mexico swearing-in ceremony for our group. The very next day, we expect to be moving to the city of Jalpan in the beautiful Sierra Gorda, where we will be living and working for the next two years. Naturally, we are looking ahead with excitement!

So please take a long look at that amazing full moon tonight. We'll be looking at it too! And if you are a mother, we are sending a sincere wish that tomorrow you will enjoy a very happy Mother's Day!

Affectionately,
Rick and Sally

# *Update 8*

## May 24, 2009
## The Beautiful Sierra Gorda

Dear family and friends:

Last Friday, we were sworn in officially as Peace Corps Mexico volunteers. The formal ceremony at the headquarters office in Querétaro was truly inspiring.

We have arrived in the beautiful Sierra Gorda! We are so excited to begin the next phase of this grand adventure! We feel privileged to begin our coming two years of service under the auspices of a US organization that seeks to develop collaboration, friendship, and peaceful relations with people in so many countries of the world.

We arrived yesterday afternoon in Jalpan de Serra and are busy organizing our new home. The house where we will be living the next two years was previously occupied by Ben and Buffy Lenth—the first Peace Corps volunteers to serve in the Sierra Gorda Biosphere Reserve. Ben and Buffy returned to the United States a couple of weeks ago. They located this house at the start of their two-year period of service and then furnished it using their Peace Corps settling-in allowance. It was a stroke of good luck that we were able to use our settling-in allowance to purchase the furniture from them. ¡Muchas gracias y buena suerte a Ben y Buffy!

Our home in Jalpan.

Our work schedule in the biosphere reserve begins bright and early tomorrow morning. Rick will share an office with our Peace Corps colleague Avram Primack, who is a GIS expert. Rick will focus on wildlife-monitoring projects and on the reserve's carbon-sequestration program.

Sally will have a desk in the library area near other staff members who work in various education projects. The reserve's Earth Center offers workshops, courses, and ecotourism activities. Some of the courses are offered online, and Sally will assist in developing course materials. She'll also help tour guides prepare and present information in English for international guests to the reserve.

In addition, Sally will be trying to build a connection between the teachers and students at the bilingual school in McKinleyville, where our grandkids Olivia and Nate attend, and a yet-to-be-identified group of teachers and students at an elementary school here in the Sierra Gorda. The school connection will fulfill another important Peace Corps Mexico goal, which is to build understanding and friendship between people in the United States and Mexico.

Attached are a few photos, including one of the swearing-in ceremony; one of Rick, Sally, and Avram with Sierra Gorda counterparts Roberto, Marina, and Víctor; and one of the US flag alongside the Peace Corps flag and the Mexican flag. Peace and friendship are worthy goals for all of us. May your hearts be filled with both!

Con cariño,
Rick and Sally

# *Update 9*

## June 7, 2009

¡Hola, familia y amigos!

We are beginning to feel somewhat integrated in our community here in Jalpan de Serra and in the community of the Sierra Gorda Biosphere Reserve. Pati Ruíz Corzo, the director of the biosphere reserve, has been very welcoming and supportive. A forthcoming article you may see in Audubon Society online materials describes an October 2010 travel opportunity in this remarkable area: http://www.travelian.com.mx/sierragorda2.html.

Rick's counterpart is Roberto Pedraza, Pati's older son. It is he who is described as the guide in the Audubon Society article. He is an amazing naturalist and guide and is committed to the success of the programs at Sierra Gorda.

Sally's counterpart is Marina Rendón, who is the coordinator of the virtual campus program within the Earth Center here. She and Pati have helped Sally understand her roles and responsibilities in relation to environmental education workshops and courses. Sally is becoming oriented to the online course Aprendiendo y Enseñando para un Futuro Sustentable, or in English, Learning and Teaching for a Sustainable Future.

Sally also has been translating Sierra Gorda descriptive materials and proposals from Spanish into English. All of these activities have reinforced her daily use of Spanish within professional and community contexts.

Rick has hired a Spanish-language professor to provide tutoring lessons, and both of us are using the Rosetta Stone curriculum—an online program provided by the Peace Corps to build on the Spanish-language skills we developed in the preservice program. Our increased fluency in Spanish will be one of the most important keys to our success here, and both of us are highly motivated!

The mission of the Sierra Gorda Biosphere Reserve is to protect, restore, and conserve this amazing region while also assisting its inhabitants to use sustainable development approaches to support themselves. Over the course of the last twenty-two years, it has been important for the reserve to compete for financial support from numerous regional, national, and international foundations and NGOs interested in promoting this valuable work.

During Sally's first week here, she enjoyed her first trip into a remote area of the reserve to visit an elementary classroom of children from six to twelve years of age in the community of Bucareli within the Pinal de Amoles region. She observed four excellent teachers from the reserve as they taught lessons and facilitated hands-on learning activities about migratory birds and the importance of protecting their habitats. The teachers used a variety of highly effective teaching tools, including physical exercises, singing, animated PowerPoint lectures, sets of binoculars and field guides for the children to observe birds in the town's central park just across the street from the school, and an art activity in which the children created colorful models of birds in flight.

This past week, she traveled to the community of La Colgada for the day with a consultant from San Francisco, California. Dorothy Yuki has served as a consultant for the reserve over the past several years. She works with women who create various products using their embroidery skills. The women market their products with support from staff in the reserve. This long-term project provides a sustainable livelihood for the women in these communities that does not involve environmental degradation, and it supports their efforts to improve and diversify their processes and products.

During both trips, Sally took photos to archive digitally. Photos from the trips included (a) a classroom at Bucareli; (b) children creating bird models; (c) Dorothy giving Blanca some sewing tips; and (d) sisters who are future embroiderers.

Rick spent the day out in the field this past week with his counterpart, Roberto, and Roberto's father, Beto, getting familiar with some of the backcountry. In addition to seeing some striking countryside, including a sinkhole 281 meters deep at the lowest part of the edge and over 400 meters high at the upper edge, he also was able to observe some male and female mountain trogons. A special treat was observing an occupied trogon nest in a rotting stump! It's the first known nest in the reserve for this particular species. Rick has been invited next Tuesday to help set up some motion-sensing cameras for detecting jaguars and other wildlife of the region. Things continue to move at a rapid pace for him too.

Today we will have another full moon in the night sky above the Sierra Gorda, and you will see that same moon above your various beautiful locations. We are thinking of you all and hoping that everything is going well in your part of the world. Let us know how you are doing!

Con cariño,
Rick and Sally

# Update 10

## June 21, 2009

¡Hola, familia y amigos!

Happy first day of summer *and* happy Father's Day to all you great fathers out there! Rick is celebrating with his kids and grandkids via a Skype connection today. Skype is a free computer download, and we absolutely love having the chance to communicate with live video and audio components every Sunday afternoon. Hooray for Skype!

This past week Sally observed a gathering of twenty-five enthusiastic participants from all over Mexico who came to the Sierra Gorda site here in Jalpan for a full week of activities, the culmination of their online diploma course, Learning and Teaching for a Sustainable Future. Last Monday and Tuesday, we traveled via the green eco-bus to a secondary school where student leaders shared the work they are doing in Ecoclubs focused on community conservation projects (a photo was attached). We also visited other community-based Sierra Gorda recycling programs that provide a solid infrastructure for collecting, sorting, consolidating, and transporting recyclables of all kinds.

During the week, participants in this innovative course enjoyed presentations about all aspects of the biosphere reserve's work in the Sierra Gorda: reforestation, restoration of soils and habitats, and production and sales of ecosystem products and services, including ecotours to pristine campgrounds, embroidery creation workshops, and carbon offset programs—to name only a few. Leaders use puppet theater and numerous songs about the environment to generate emotional and spiritual connections with Mother Earth. Maestra Pati plays her accordion and leads groups in singing all their favorites (see photo).

The week ended with an evening premiere showing of the amazing documentary *Home* by Yann Arthus-Bertand (narrated in Spanish by Salma Hayek and in English by Glenn Close). The film is available online at http://www.yannarthusbertrand.org/en/films-tv/home.

Rick has been working on translations of key reports from Spanish into English that are intended for international supporters of work in the reserve. The translation work also serves to inform Rick about the various biosphere programs. He is becoming more involved in the carbon offset program in which members of the local and, often, poorer communities are paid for the ecological services that result from their use of good environmental practices such as sustainable forestry, controlled cattle grazing, and soil and water restoration and conservation.

Rick will be a liaison between the Sierra Gorda Biosphere Reserve and potential donors who are interested in supporting these practices. This particular reserve program is resulting in improved habitat protection and preservation of the Sierra Gorda region; sustainable development; reduction of poverty in the local communities; increased support by the local people for sound, sustainable ecological practices; and opportunities for individuals and agencies to make donations while raising their profiles as supporters of healthy long-term ecological practices. Obviously, a good program at several levels!

Rick also enjoys his wildlife fieldwork with a local landowner along with his counterpart, Roberto Pedraza, who is doing the primary monitoring of wildlife biodiversity in the Sierra Gorda, and Juan Cruzado, another Sierra Gorda colleague. Heat- and motion-sensing wildlife cameras have been put in place. Juan attracted several ticks, which Rick preserved and mailed for identification to Rick Brown, a colleague at Humboldt State who is an expert. If you would like to see one of Rick's tick pics, just let him know at botzlerr@sbcglobal.net.

Good wishes to all of you from both of us. We hope that you are doing well and that you will give us periodic updates on your experiences too!

Con cariño,
Rick and Sally

# *Update 11*

## July 4, 2009

¡Hola, familia y amigos!

We hope that those of you in the United States are enjoying your celebrations of Independence Day today! Happy Fourth of July!

Here in Mexico, the biggest fiesta of the year is the nation's own Independence Day on September 16. Next year, in 2010, Mexico will focus on its bicentennial celebration of its independence from the rule of Spain and the one hundredth anniversary of its revolution. Following is an interesting excerpt, in English, from the website *Explorando México*.

Mexico is getting ready for an extraordinary celebration in honor of its 200th anniversary of its Independence and 100th anniversary of its Revolution. Everything designed to commemorate these two great dates is linked to the ideal of renewing Mexico's identity and historic continuity.

Highlighted among the many projects are exhibits of prehispanic, Spanish, modern and contemporary Mexican art at the most important capitals of the world, historic routes, shows, publications, seminars, the opening of 10 new archeological sites, maintenance to the country's most important prehispanic sites and the remodeling of 30 museums that will serve as venues to the Independence's Bicentennial and the Revolution's Centennial in the year 2010.

This work involves a complex museography and the consolidation of historic buildings in six States to commemorate the Independence and in eight States to commemorate the Revolution, with a budget of over 300 million pesos.

The venues were chosen by taking into consideration their accessibility by land, routes that go over the steps of those who fought the battles that concluded in the consummation of Mexico's Independence and Revolution. For this great celebration, these routes combined are known as "Ruta 2010," for which the Ministry of Communication and Transportation will destine its resources for signaling these roads and provide tourism information in print at strategic points of the highways and through its website.

The museums highlighted along the Route of Independence start with Casa del Marques at Mexico City's Historic Center and in Acapulco with the San Diego Fort Museum, where Morelos fought his famous battle for the country's Independence. Other venue museums in this celebration chosen for their priceless content in honor of these two unforgettable dates are Museum of the Viceroyalty, the National Anthropology Museum, the National History Museum, the Allende Museum, The Casa Morelos Museum, Alhóndiga de Granaditas and the Museum at the Home of Father Hidalgo.

The Independence road includes the Freedom Route, traveling on the footsteps of Miguel Hidalgo y Costilla from Corralejo in Guanajuato to Chihuahua, passing by Querétaro and Michoacán.

If you would like to read more, the *Explorando México* website is at http://www.explorandomexico. com/about-mexico/11/280/.

Both the state and the city of Querétaro are gearing up for the historical celebration. We look forward to learning more history about this region, state, and country in the months ahead.

We hope you all have a safe, enjoyable, and relaxing Fourth of July!

Con cariño,
Rick and Sally

# *Update 12*

## July 26, 2009

¡Hola, familia y amigos!

Here in Mexico there is a special phrase of hospitality and welcome: "¡mi casa es tu casa!"—"my house is your house!" In a slight adaptation, we welcome *you* to our home in Jalpan de Serra in the beautiful Sierra Gorda: our house is your house, nuestra casa es su casa. So if you are planning a trip to Mexico, please visit us!

As we recently wrote to former PCVs Ben and Buffy Lenth, who lived and worked here in the Sierra Gorda the previous two years, the two of us are slowly but surely settling into a routine. We are enjoying the process of getting to know people here in Jalpan and in the Sierra Gorda office. Our work lives during the week are very busy.

Our adobe-style home has thick walls that insulate well against the heat. The house is in the central district of Jalpan, just a couple of blocks from the beautiful mission church. The attached photo was taken against a cloudy summer sky.

Mission church in Jalpan.

The thunder and lightning storms during the summer months here are something to behold, and the rain pours furiously from those magnificent clouds. Though it's generally hot and humid here right now, the rains freshen and cool the air, and it becomes quite pleasant.

Throughout the summer, the huge mango tree in our yard has been bursting with fruit, and ripe mangos fall intermittently, day and night. We have been enjoying the sweet mangos a lot and have been sharing containers of them with several folks since there is such an abundance of the juicy fruit.

Nearly every week, we enjoy fresh papaya from the tree in our yard too, and one of the several young banana trees is budding. The birds also are attracted to the ripe papayas!

The two of us often comment on how fortunate we are to have been able to move into the home the Lenths occupied. It has been very convenient to have a fully furnished place and sometimes a delightful surprise to discover something we initially overlooked, like the little vacuum cleaner on the top shelf of the storage closet.

Our wonderful landlady, Angélica, is always very thoughtful and kind. And her brother Mario, who operates a hardware store just a few doors down from us, has been supportive and helpful too. Across the street at the little general store, where we routinely buy our drinking water, we have developed a cordial relationship with Ephraim, a kindly old gentleman.

And the children in the area are responding with twinkles in their eyes to our persistent "¡Buenos días!" y "¡Hola!" Hopefully, they are getting used to our American accents.

We are so glad the Lenths recommended that we hire someone to help with the cleaning, even though our Peace Corps stipend is limited. Siria de Fuentes now works for us every Saturday morning for four hours of general cleaning—mostly sweeping, dusting the furniture, cleaning the bathroom, and mopping all the floors. Wow, in only a week's time, everything gets *so* dusty!

Siria is hardworking, and she takes great pride in the quality of her work. We also enjoy our conversations with her, and she is very patient with our efforts to express ourselves comprehensibly in Spanish. Her young teenage daughter Pati came to meet us one Saturday. Pati will be starting high school in the fall, and she enjoys her studies and school activities a lot. She is friendly and articulate, and she and her mother obviously have a close bond. Having Siria work for us also is mutually beneficial: we have the extra help we need, and Siria has a little added income for her family.

With an open-air kitchen, our home naturally has its share of little creatures. We are greeted daily by the chirping of birds and by the chirping of the small lizards and skinks that do their best to scurry out of sight. Little rose-bellied lizards (*Sceloporus variabilis*, or *lagartija-escamosa panza rosada* in Spanish) regularly sun themselves on the stone walkway in our garden.

Siria discovered a scorpion in a dark corner of the living room when she was sweeping last week. After showing it to us, she dispatched it with the end of the broom. This variety of scorpion has a painful sting but is otherwise harmless. We know that Albert Schweitzer would have reverenced the lives of *all* the creatures here, but ...

Of course, the occasional *cucaracha* makes an appearance too. (We don't use the English word for *cucaracha* in our home.) Since Sally has a strong aversion, Rick purchased a metal spatula with which he is quite deft at efficiently terminating (whacking) these unwelcome guests. One afternoon, when Rick was not home, Sally grabbed the spatula and slammed a poor creature with such force that the spatula broke into bits. Rick bought a sturdier one.

Rick finally took the suggestion of Ben, who used to walk up Benito Juárez (our street) into the hills with his dog Chavo, to see where our road really ends. Rick started on our street (the Benito Juárez School is just to the right of the church) and walked west to the end, which was at kilometer marker 175 on Mexico Highway 120. He then followed a road (that became a trail) parallel to the highway, which eventually merged with the highway in the quaint town of Puerto de Animas ("Refuge of the Soul").

Along the way Rick managed to see his first road runner (*Geococcyx californianus*; *correcaminos* in Spanish) and came upon a group of six or seven black vultures (*Coragyps atratus*; *zopilotes* in Spanish) roosting in a grove of trees; they took considerable exception to his presence before lifting off to catch the local air currents. Rick also managed to see and greet many friendly people working in the fields along the way. The whole trip was about six miles direct round trip, but with a little extra for exploring some side trails. It was a nice introduction to some of the local habitats and vistas.

Yesterday evening, we enjoyed going to the local community Festival of Santiago (St. James, in English). The evening included traditional Huastecan music, a contemporary band from Querétaro, and a spectacular fireworks display. It was especially fun to be among so many happy people of all ages dancing in the streets.

You may have read that returned Peace Corps volunteer Aaron Williams has been nominated as the eighteenth Peace Corps director. A well-written article about the nomination is at http://www.iscvt.org/news/articles/article/?id=53. Williams served in the Dominican Republic in 1967–1970, and he is fluent in Spanish. The relatively new Peace Corps Mexico program will have strong support when Williams's nomination is confirmed.

Once again, please know that *nuestra casa es su casa*. If you would like more information about how to get to Jalpan de Serra in the amazing Sierra Gorda, please let us know. It would be a pleasure to introduce you to our Mexican colleagues and friends and to the wonders of the biosphere reserve.

Affectionately,
Rick and Sally

# *Update 13*

## August 22, 2009

¡Hola, familia y amigos!

These last few weeks, our lives here in the Sierra Gorda have been filled with a wide variety of enriching cultural, language, and work-related experiences—both in the reserve's offices and in some of the surrounding natural areas. Margarita Pedraza Muñoz oversees the reserve's ecotourism sites as well as its collaborative work with local artisans who craft a wide range of appealing products.

Margarita took us on hikes to the Escanela River with its stunning Puente de Dios (http:// sierragordaecotours.com/sitios-a-visitar/destinos-detalle.php?destino=9) and to San Juan de los Durán with its breathtaking vistas of mountains, valleys, and dense forests (http:// sierragordaecotours.com/sitios-a-visitar/destinos-detalle.php?destino=35&lang=en).

Today, we'll be hiking with Margarita in the Ayutla area (http://sierragordaecotours.com/ sitios-a-visitar/destinos-detalle.php?destino=17&lang=es).

Both of us also have attended weeklong Peace Corps workshops—Sally as part of a monitoring and evaluation working group and Rick as part of a biodiversity monitoring group. We have appreciated the well-organized professional development opportunities Peace Corps Mexico continuously provides us as volunteers as well as the chance to reconnect with colleagues and share experiences.

Sally also recently attended a three-day Sierra Gorda workshop titled "Paths to Sustainability," facilitated by five inspiring people from Mexico, Peru, and France who are involved with projects related to social entrepreneurship as part of their affiliation with the international Ashoka organization (https://www.ashoka.org/en). The reserve's director, Pati Ruíz Corzo, was selected as an Ashoka fellow in 1996 for her innovative approach to conservation of a natural protected area, through strategies that actively engage the local population of Sierra Gorda residents and that support them in changing traditional practices damaging to the environment to conservation-oriented activities that promote sustainable social and economic development while eradicating poverty.

The culmination of the workshop was a hike to a summit in Cuatro Palos, where the group took time to behold the grandeur of the ancient mountain range with its distinctive Media Luna formation (http://sierragordaecotours.com/sitios-a-visitar/destinos-detalle.php?destino=4). All the while, a plucky swift continuously circled above the group members' heads at breakneck speeds, perhaps in an effort to distract us from its nearby nest.

Beginning August 31, Sally also will be enrolling in the Sierra Gorda online course Teaching and Learning for a Sustainable Future, which integrates an adaptation of the UNESCO curriculum based on the United Nations' Decade of Education for Sustainable Development (for information on UNESCO's work, see http://www.un.org/sustainabledevelopment/). It is fascinating to be learning about the concept of sustainable development within the context of the Sierra Gorda Biosphere Reserve, which is a remarkable living example of these ideas.

Last Saturday, August 15, we traveled down to Querétaro to attend the baptism of little Isabella, one of the granddaughters in our Castrejón-Ángeles host family there. The beautiful church was filled to standing-room-only capacity as several families gathered with their little ones for the baptismal service. The priest gave a homily that captured the importance of the rite while adding the humor and warmth needed to help the intergenerational congregation feel at home together as they celebrated the special occasion. Young Isabella was with her parents Toño and Lisbeth during her baptism, and she looked radiant.

Following the service, all of Isabella's family, including both sets of grandparents and all of her aunts and uncles and cousins, gathered for a festive dinner celebration at a garden location that included both indoor and outdoor play areas for the myriad children to enjoy. The built-in trampoline was a big hit and allowed some of the more experienced kids to demonstrate their skills with well-executed backflips. We felt privileged to be invited to the baptism and family festivities, and our Spanish conversations boosted our confidence in our growing sense of cultural integration here in Mexico.

Following Isabella's baptism, Sally returned to the Sierra Gorda reserve while Rick remained in Querétaro to attend the biodiversity monitoring workshop sponsored by Peace Corps Mexico. It was an excellent opportunity for him to meet other professional biologists and ecologists of Mexico who were working in protected areas or national forests, as well as the PC volunteers working on these sites. Discussions included the role of monitoring biodiversity in understanding Mexico's biological and ecological treasures and how the knowledge from these studies can be applied to better address habitat restoration and enhancement for vulnerable species of plants and animals.

Please let us know how *you* are doing. We really enjoy news from family and friends. Our best wishes to you all!

Con cariño,
Rick and Sally

# *Update 14*

## September 16, 2009
## Mexican Independence Day

¡Hola, familia y amigos!

Today is Independence Day in Mexico, and here in Jalpan the festivities began yesterday evening under rainy skies. Though many of us used umbrellas, the off-and-on showers didn't dampen the spirits of the huge crowd gathered to enjoy the start of the national holiday with a few hours of music and dancing.

There was a fabulous Huastecan Huapango trio who played their stringed instruments and sang their hearts out while couples executed the dance steps in perfect synchrony with the beat. See the YouTube demo from Veracruz at http://www.youtube.com/watch?v=zTBiDW6vJ6E. Our friends Paul, Margarita, and Bibiana also enjoyed a couple of hours of Huapango dancing in our kitchen one evening.

A dance troupe from the state of Jalisco also performed several folk dances, dressed in traditional colorful attire. The women's flying skirts and men's large hats accentuated their perfect execution of the well-known folk songs.

The evening ended at 11:00 p.m. with the customary *grito*, in which all of us joined in enthusiastic shouts of "¡Viva Mexico!" Many then dispersed while others celebrated into the night.

At 8:00 a.m. this morning, families gathered in the central garden near the Jalpan mission for the children's parade, which featured boys and girls of all ages—from every preschool, elementary school, and high school in the area—dressed in their school uniforms and marching in unison. School bands and their directors led the way, with students marching while skillfully playing their drums and trumpets.

The morning was very well organized with formal presentations, honor guards, the singing of the national anthem, and introductions of dignitaries. The children were very well behaved and attentive. At the end, lunches were distributed to all of the children, and families sat together in the garden enjoying the time together.

We took many photos that captured the celebration. It was a memorable occasion and one more opportunity for us to better understand and appreciate the beautiful Mexican spirit. The partly cloudy weather was perfect for the occasion, *and* there was no rain on this parade!

Next year will be the bicentennial celebration of Mexico's independence (1810–2010). And 2010 also will be the one hundredth anniversary of the revolution. So we will be here in Mexico during a particularly festive year with a wide variety of cultural and historical activities to commemorate it—a great year for *you* to visit us in Mexico too!

Good wishes to you all from the two of us in Jalpan de Serra in the heart of the beautiful Sierra Gorda Biosphere Reserve, Querétaro, Mexico.

Con cariño,
Rick and Sally

# *Update 15*

## October 17, 2009

¡Hola, familia y amigos!

It's another rainy Saturday here in Jalpan, and we have hung our laundry in the open-air kitchen rather than in the yard. Rick has mounted clotheslines that can easily be extended and connected in both places and then taken down once the clothes are dry.

On rainy days, with humidity at 100 percent, it takes a while longer for the clothes to dry—sometimes two days! We welcome the rain and all it adds to the lushness and beauty of the Sierra. Last weekend, we went with friends to the Chuveje waterfall, which was a sight to behold, with water gushing wildly into a stream that feeds the Jalpan River.

We will be attending a regional Peace Corps meeting tomorrow (Sunday) afternoon in Xilitla in the nearby state of San Luis Potosí. Then, on Tuesday, we will travel to Querétaro for the weeklong Peace Corps Mexico "reconnect" meeting for our group—returning to Jalpan next Sunday, October 24. It will be fun to see the staff and our colleagues as well as to pay a visit to our host family there—we'll be seeing Lupe and Antonio on Tuesday evening. As an extension of the meeting, there will be an "all volunteer" gathering on Friday and Saturday for currently serving volunteers in the country. It's hard to believe we've been here in Mexico almost eight months!

With the assistance of Lulú Benítez Rubio and Olivia Pérez Jiménez, leaders in Sierra Gorda's Community Environmental Education program, our plans for making connections between students at our grandchildren's bilingual elementary school in McKinleyville, California, and children at the Benito Juárez primary school here in Jalpan de Serra, Querétaro, are coming together.

Jalpan school bulletin board.

We soon will be matching the children and beginning the correspondence exchange. Sally is working with first- and second-grade teachers for the exchange program, and Rick is collaborating with fourth-grade teachers using the Birds Beyond Borders program as a focus.

Along with visiting Peace Corps trainee JoElla Jackson-Tyree, Sally recently enjoyed observing Lulú as she gave professional development presentations to groups of preschool teachers and their program coordinators. Lulú taught lively Sierra Gorda songs (accompanying herself on guitar), and she demonstrated a variety of age-appropriate environmental education activities that the teachers can readily adapt for use with the young children in their preschools.

As you may know, the International Day of Climate Action is Saturday, October 24 (during our time in Querétaro). As reported by the Communication Initiative Network, this is "the date set for worldwide rallies and symbolic actions to highlight the importance of 350 parts per million (ppm) as the level scientists have identified as the safe upper limit for carbon dioxide ($CO_2$) in the earth's atmosphere. (Currently, the atmosphere measures just over 390 ppm, and the level is rising by 2 ppm per year)."

The Communication Initiative Network (http://www.comminit.com/en/node/303007/36) provides this explanation:

> The movement to take one day and use it to stop the climate crisis has been launched by '350.org,' a global network formed in 2008 to connect people around the world who are united by a common call to action: the world, they say, needs a fair international climate treaty to reach 350. "We're calling on people around the world to organize an action on October 24 incorporating the number 350

at an iconic place in their community, and then upload a photo of their event to 350.org website. We'll collect these images from around the world and, with your help, deliver them to the media and world leaders. Together, we can show our world and its decision-makers just how big, beautiful, and unified the climate movement really is." The goal is to leverage October 24 as a day of action for meaningful political change.

The Sierra Gorda Biosphere Reserve will hold its 350 Day of Climate Action event on Friday, October 23, in the central park in Jalpan. We will be attending a Peace Corps Mexico meeting that day but hope to join with others in Querétaro celebrating this national call to action. In one of the activities this week in the Sierra Gorda online course Sally is taking, Teaching and Learning for a Sustainable Future, participants each calculated their own "ecological footprint." Sally calculated both her footprint as a Peace Corps volunteer in Mexico and her footprint as a retired educator in California. Very different results! If you'd like to calculate your ecological footprint using this same instrument, it is at http://www.myfootprint.org/.

The reserve publishes monthly bulletins that detail progress on its goals. See https://vivasierragorda.wordpress.com/category/news-from-the-sierra-gorda/.

The two of us have begun the process of making connections between the Sierra Gorda reserve and university programs in the United States. Earlier this month, an initial contact was made with Jim Howard, dean of the College of Natural Resources and Sciences, Humboldt State University, and Carl Hanson, director of extended education at HSU. Our hope is that in the near future the unique treasures of the Sierra Gorda and the reserve's innovative programs aimed at enhancing both the environment and the social and economic well-being of the people living here will become the focus of studies and field experiences among university faculty and students.

Well, Rick is getting himself into some major trouble this next month. For some reason, he thought a good way to connect with other professional colleagues in Mexico would be to attend a professional meeting or two. He even thought in a moment of madness, *Maybe I'll submit an abstract for a professional presentation.* He accidentally submitted two, and (gulp) both of them were accepted.

The first paper, "*Batrachochytrium dendrobatidis*: Un riesgo potencialmente grave para los anfibios de México" (roughly translated, "*Batrachochytrium dendrobatidis*: A Potentially Serious Risk to Amphibians of Mexico"), has been accepted for an oral presentation at the Primer Congreso en Ecología de Enfermedades y Medicina de la Conservación Kalaankab (First Congress on Disease Ecology and Conservation Medicine, Kalaankab), November 4–7, 2009, at the Universidad Veracruzana, Puerto de Veracruz, Mexico.

The other paper, "Perspectivas éticas y su relación con programas de conservación de la Biodiversidad" ("Ethical Perspectives and Their Relation to Biodiversity Programs"), has been accepted for an oral presentation at the Encuentro Nacional sobre Biodiversidad, Conservación, y Restauración Ecológica en México (National Meeting on Biodiversity, Conservation, and Ecological Restoration in Mexico), November 17–19, 2009, in Morelia Michoacán, Mexico.

Both papers, of course, will need to be presented in Spanish—this from a person who isn't even sure he knows enough Spanish to travel safely by bus to either site! Talk about increasingly sleepless nights. What could he have been thinking?

We thoroughly enjoyed collaborating with Laurita Dominguez Loyola, a good friend of Ben and Buffy Lenth (the Peace Corps couple who preceded us here in the Sierra Gorda), in hosting a virtual baby shower (*lluvia virtual*) last week, using Skype via computer to connect live with Ben and Buffy in Colorado.

Ben and Buffy Lenth's baby is due at the beginning of November. During the shower, the Lenths and their dog Chavo had the chance for personal communications with many of their Mexican friends, and they also participated in the entertaining games Laurita had planned. It was a blast!

You may enjoy seeing the YouTube video of new Peace Corps director Aaron Williams as he addressed the community of volunteers serving around the world. We feel fortunate to have a director who is a returned volunteer himself, having served in the Dominican Republic in 1967–1970, and who is fluent in Spanish. The video is located at http://www.youtube.com/ watch?v=Faa-rfULmXM. His message is inspiring.

We look forward to attending the fiftieth anniversary of Peace Corps in Washington, DC, September 20–25, 2011.The events will be held the fall after we return to California. This celebration should be especially meaningful for us following our Peace Corps Mexico experience.

We are sending our warmest wishes to each and every one of you. When you have a little time, please fill us in on the latest news in your lives!

Con cariño,
Rick and Sally

# *Update 16*

## November 2, 2009

¡Hola, familia y amigos!

Yesterday was All Saints Day, and here in Mexico and throughout Latin America, people also celebrated el Día de los Muertos (the Day of the Dead). We attended some of the festivities here in Jalpan and were impressed with the loving remembrances assembled in beautifully decorated altars at many locations in the community—most with bright bouquets or woven strands of orange, yellow, and gold marigolds, the traditional flower for the occasion. The two of us took time to share some of our own fond memories of our parents and grandparents with one another.

At a friend's home yesterday, we were invited for a delicious Day of the Dead meal of tamales and other special foods and beverages. Today we attended the Catholic mass at the community cemetery, where hundreds of families came to honor their loved ones. The graves were tended and decorated with flowers and candles, and people of all ages, from babies and small children to the very elderly and infirm, gathered at the family plots throughout the service, which included a full liturgy, sermon, and communion service under ancient trees with a deep blue sky overhead.

To learn about the history and cultural traditions of the Day of the Dead, you might enjoy reading some of the articles available at planeta.com. The lead article focuses on the holiday here in Mexico and includes examples of traditions, art, and other distinctive features of the celebration: http://www.planeta.com/ecotravel/mexico/mexdead.html.

Tonight Rick is leaving on the evening bus for Veracruz, where he will be presenting a talk at the Primer Congreso en Ecología de Enfermedades y Medicina de la Conservación Kalaankab (First Congress on Disease Ecology and Conservation Medicine, Kalaankab). Just this morning, he was contacted via e-mail by the president of the group and asked to give a second presentation related to some of his professional work in wildlife diseases. Needless to say, Rick is *muy emocionado y poco nervioso* (very excited and a little nervous). Or maybe he is *poco emocionado y muy nervioso*!

Anyway, he'll be back home here in Jalpan on Saturday, November 7, and then nine days later he'll take off for the conference in Morelia Michoacán, Mexico, where he'll be giving an ethical perspectives presentation. Sally won't be accompanying him to either conference due to her own busy schedule with Sierra Gorda, but she's glad that Rick will be here with her on November 15 to celebrate forty-six years of wedded bliss. Really—forty-six years!

Many thanks to all of you who have sent us a note or two during our time here! It is always wonderful to hear from you. All the best to each and every one of you!

Con cariño,
Rick and Sally

# *Update 17*

## November 26, 2009
## ¡Feliz Día de Acción de Gracias! Happy Thanksgiving Day!

For November 26, 2009

Dear family and friends:

In the United States, tomorrow is Thanksgiving Day. Of course, every day there are so many blessings for which we give thanks. However, this is a good day to take the opportunity to give thanks to each of you for your great support of us during our period of service as volunteers in Peace Corps Mexico.

It is an honor and privilege to be here in Jalpan de Serra working with the personnel of the Sierra Gorda Biosphere Reserve of Querétaro. As we have mentioned in the past, we are very impressed with the vision, mission, and passion of the leaders and staff on behalf of Mother Earth and their commitment to improving the environment and the well-being of the people who live here in a unique "conservation economy" that seeks sustainable development for the environment and for the people. Their program is sure to be replicated successfully worldwide.

We also appreciate the Peace Corps México (PCM) personnel in Querétaro and in Washington, DC, especially those in our PCM environment program. Ángel Piñeda, Benita Luna, and Beatriz Charles, along with all the other leaders, coordinators, and staff, have extended strong encouragement and many kindnesses to us both during our preservice programs and now during our period of service. We are very grateful for their professional and friendly support.

Again, many thanks to each of you for your support and for your ongoing interest in our Peace Corps experience. Happy Thanksgiving Day to everyone!

Affectionately,
Rick y Sally

# *Update 18*

## February 1, 2010

¡Hola, familia y amigos!

As Peace Corps volunteers, we are continuing to become more integrated and involved with the remarkable work of Grupo Ecológico in the Sierra Gorda Biosphere Reserve, in the northern part of the state of Querétaro. Rick has begun participating in the training program for young ecotourism guides at Cuatro Palos, a community about fifty-five kilometers southwest of Jalpan.

Cuatro Palos historically has not had a strong economic base and often has lost its young people to bigger cities such as Querétaro, where they have sought employment opportunities. However, Cuatro Palos is set in some remarkable natural beauty. For example, the Media Luna view from the town is extraordinary.

Media Luna in Cuatro Palos.

In an effort to strengthen the economic base of the area, Grupo Ecológico has helped the community establish an ecotourism program. As part of this process, interested youth are being trained as guides, with seven currently in the program. Ranging in age from eight to fourteen years old, they already have considerable knowledge about the ecology, geology, and culture of their region and are very enthusiastic about this program, which holds great promise for strengthening the economic and social well-being of the community.

Shortly after our return from a two-week holiday vacation in California, a cold front hit much of Mexico. One of the surprises we subsequently encountered here in the Sierra Gorda was snow! On the sixteenth of January, one of the normal training days for the Cuatro Palos guides, enough snow had fallen that the roads were closed, leaving the town and neighboring communities cut off from the main highway for a while.

Rick and one of the staff members walked the four miles up to the community, enjoying the views of children taking delight in this unexpected opportunity as well as seeing the semidesert plants in snow! It was a pleasant surprise to see this region of Mexico in a little different light!

On another note, with support from the director and key staff of the biosphere reserve, Rick is planning a small study to evaluate local amphibians for the presence and distribution of a fungus adversely affecting amphibians in many regions of the world. As some of you know, *Batrachochytrium dendrobatidis* is linked to the declines and extinction of over two hundred species of amphibians. Dr. Gabriela Parra Olea, of the Universidad Nacional Autónoma de México, has been a primary researcher in understanding the role of this fungus in Mexico and will evaluate samples that Rick will collect from the Sierra Gorda as part of her study on the role of *B. dendrobatidis* in Mexico.

The fungus has been reported in eight of the states of Mexico, but there has not yet been any work in the state of Querétaro—including the Sierra Gorda. Rick is hoping to gain a small amount of funding from the Peace Corps to offset some costs of this study.

One last little bit of news from Rick is that he has begun letting his beard grow again! It has been a very long while and, of course, will be dependent on whether he can put up with the lengthy process. However, if he decides to continue, a big question will be whether there is any red remaining in the field of white that surely will emerge. Only time will tell!

Sally has nearly finished the fifteen-week Sierra Gorda online diploma course Teaching and Learning for a Sustainable Future (Enseñando y Aprendiendo para un Futuro Sustentable), which is offered only in Spanish. The additional week of required on-site activities here in Jalpan de Serra is scheduled for this week (February 2–5, 2010).

Conversing face-to-face with the other course participants will provide an excellent opportunity for further language development on topics directly connected to our work as Peace Corps Mexico volunteers in the reserve. Rick is planning to take this course when it is offered again starting in April.

The two of us also are working to develop university connections between the reserve and Humboldt State University (HSU) in Northern California, where we served as professors for many years. At present, we are beginning to develop a three-week course in English that we hope can be offered through HSU's Extended Education Sierra Institute in summer 2011.

This course will involve students in actively learning about the biosphere reserve's work in sustainable development. We are very excited! In addition, we are collaborating with the reserve staff in designing ecotourism activities for an international, English-speaking audience that we hope will be approved by Exploritas International (part of Elderhostel).

Partly due to the desire to reach out to international visitors, Sally recently was asked to organize English-language classes for Sierra Gorda staff. She is looking forward to working in this special way with some of the reserve's personnel—including ecotourism guides.

Sally's work in translating many of the reserve's documents from Spanish to English will allow her to tailor the classes to the context of the reserve's programs. This should help keep the content relevant and interesting.

We now have successfully launched the correspondence exchange program between children in primary classes at the Benito Juárez School here in Jalpan and those at Morris School in McKinleyville, California—our hometown. We believe that this project has great potential for fulfilling part of the Peace Corps mission to help "promote a better understanding of the American people on the part of the people served," as well to help the children and families at Morris develop a better understanding of the people here in Mexico.

As we mentioned in a past update, Morris School has a bilingual Spanish-immersion program, and two of our grandchildren, Nate and Olivia, are enrolled there in the first and second grades, respectively. Sally is working with these lower grades, and Rick is working with teachers at the fourth-grade level using the international Birds Beyond Borders program, known as Aves Sin Fronteras in Spanish. The correspondence between children at all grade levels is in Spanish—one great advantage.

The exchange program has taken a good deal of time to reach this point and has benefited from the support here in Jalpan of two environmental education leaders in the reserve's Community Environmental Education program. Ernestina (Lulú) Benítez Rubio and Olivia Pérez Jiménez accompanied us to potential school sites in Jalpan, introduced us to directors, and offered feedback on our materials, as we requested. Their assistance was invaluable.

Likewise, the principal at Morris School, Michael Davies-Hughes, has been a constant source of encouragement and support and has done his best to share information about our Peace Corps project with the teachers and students at his school site. In addition, we recruited our two daughters, Emi and Sarah (the mothers of Olivia and Nate), to pick up and mail packets of letters and to do any duplicating needed—great family support for their Peace Corps parents!

We really appreciate the interest and support of all of you who have asked to be on this mailing list for periodic updates. Muchas gracias to everyone! When you have a moment, please let us know how *you* are doing too!

Con cariño,
Rick and Sally

# *Update 19*

## May 5, 2010
## Cinco de Mayo

¡Hola, familia y amigos!

We are very excited about sharing the link to the brand-new website for the Sierra Gorda Biosphere Reserve here in Querétaro, Mexico: www.sierragorda.net. We think that you will enjoy exploring the various sections of the new site with their beautiful photographs and up-to-date descriptions of the reserve's work in the region.

As noted in the most recent Sierra Gorda newsletter, as of April 1 there was a change in the administration of the biosphere reserve. Pati Ruíz Corzo has led the reserve's efforts for over twenty-two years and has been the government-appointed director for the past thirteen years. The record of accomplishments under her leadership is impressive. Pati will continue as director of the Sierra Gorda Ecological Group and its Alliance for the Conservation of the Sierra Gorda. However, the new director for the Mexican federal government's National Commission of Natural Protected Areas here at the reserve is Víctor Ildefonso, who has served as sub-director under Pati's leadership for many years.

We continue to feel very grateful to be able to work as Peace Corps Mexico volunteers here in the Sierra Gorda and to be observing Pati's dynamic and dedicated efforts in promoting sustainable development and a conservation economy, which have achieved so much toward the restoration and preservation of the natural environment while improving the social and economic well-being of local people.

Coincidentally, at the beginning of April, the Peace Corps Mexico program welcomed its new country director, Daniel Evans. Outgoing director Byron Battle began the Mexico program in 2004 and provided the leadership to establish a strong Peace Corps presence here. We have been grateful for Byron's support and have appreciated the hospitality and kindness that he and his wife Margarita have extended to all of the PCVs here in Mexico.

We look forward to becoming acquainted with Dan and his wife Julia as they become part of the PC Mexico community. In fact, their first visit to the Sierra Gorda has been scheduled for May 12–15, and we are pleased that they will be staying with us in our home in Jalpan for the visit.

In a Peace Corps Mexico newsletter article, Dan was introduced by former country director Byron Battle, who said, "We all are extremely lucky to have Dan Evans on board as we enter a major growth period for Peace Corps Mexico."

Over the past few weeks, we have participated in several events celebrated either nationally or internationally. Since 1924 here in Mexico, April 30 has been designated as el Día del Niño (observations of Children's Day in other countries are described at Wikipedia at http://en.wikipedia.

org/wiki/Children's Day). Sally took a few photos of the fiesta at the school here in Jalpan where we have set up the pen-pal exchange program connecting with the bilingual elementary school in California that two of our grandchildren attend (Olivia and Nate).

Although children in Mexico usually are neatly attired in school uniforms, on the Day of the Child, they are permitted to wear "regular" clothes, and their parents and teachers decorate the school with colorful crepe paper and balloons and organize activities and refreshments that appeal to the children— who obviously feel appreciated!

Also mentioned in the Sierra Gorda newsletter, on April 22 the fortieth anniversary of international Earth Day was celebrated here in Jalpan. The Sierra Gorda Ecological Group sponsored activities in the central garden that were attended by children, youth, and families from the area. Organized by Ernestina (Lulú) Benítez Rubio, who is the head of the Sierra Gorda Community Environmental Education program, the event featured some of the songs and dances frequently taught to schoolchildren in the various communities, a dance by a group of women from Purísima de Arista, and a performance by a children's group from Tilaco honoring St. Francis of Assisi.

It is hard for us to believe that we have completed half of our twenty-seven-month period of Peace Corps service here in Mexico and that we will be attending our midservice events in Querétaro on May 16–21. Our lives as volunteers have been challenging, enlightening, productive, enjoyable, and very educational.

We are continuing to learn from the experience, and we are certain that it has enhanced our lives immeasurably. If any of you are inclined to consider Peace Corps service, please let us know. We'd be happy to share our experiences with you.

We hope that each of you is doing well. Please send us an update on what's going on in your lives. We always love to get news from family and friends.

Con cariño,
Rick and Sally

# *Update 20*

## June 2010

¡Hola, familia y amigos!

The most recent *News Bulletin from the Alliance for the Conservation of the Sierra Gorda Biosphere Reserve Querétaro* described all of its latest events. Rick enjoyed videotaping the Seventh National Ecoclub Camp-Out last weekend, and one of his videos appeared in an article. Rick now is in the process of editing all of the videos he took.

The two of us are impressed with the Ecoclubs of the Sierra Gorda and their support of youth leadership development in promoting all aspects of school and community environmental responsibility. When we return to California, we plan to explore the possibility of establishing an Ecoclub for youth in our area. (At this time, there are no Ecoclubs in the United States.)

It's almost summertime, and we are very excited that a number of our children and grandchildren are able to join us for a week of vacation here in Mexico. They soon will be flying into Guadalajara, and we will be traveling from there to Lake Chapala—Mexico's largest natural lake—and to Zacatecas, a center of historical and cultural significance. It will be so much fun to be together!

Next time, be prepared for a slew of vacation photos!

Con cariño,
Rick y Sally

# *Update 21*

## July 4, 2010
## Happy Independence Day!

¡Hola, familia y amigos!

We returned from our family vacation in Guadalajara, Lake Chapala, and Zacatecas last weekend, and everyone had a great time. It was so much fun for us simply to have our children and grandchildren with us in Mexico and to share some time with them.

Although not everyone could come, there were fifteen of us. Interestingly, when we asked about everyone's favorite part of the vacation, the hotel swimming pool in Guadalajara was one of the biggest hits!

We hope you are enjoying a festive, safe, and relaxing Fourth of July!

Con cariño,
Rick y Sally

# Update 22

## July 6, 2010

¡Hola, familia y amigos!

The English version of the current bulletin from the Alliance for the Conservation of the Sierra Gorda Biosphere Reserve, Querétaro, was just released.

An online article titled "Conservation Can Be a Weapon against Poverty" also was posted yesterday at http://www.guardian.co.uk/environment/2010/jul/05/conservation-poverty-sierra-gorda. Based on her interviews of leaders in the reserve, author Daniela Pastrana reports about "how local people can be paid for protecting their environment." The article provides a thought-provoking summary of the reserve's unique approach to sustainable development with a "conservation economy."

As the school year in the Sierra Gorda region draws to an end, we are feeling a sense of deep satisfaction about the international exchange activities we've facilitated between classes of students in the elementary schools here in Jalpan de Serra and in McKinleyville, California, our hometown. We have worked with teachers and students at two primary schools in Jalpan, Benito Juárez and Melchor Ocampo, connecting them with Morris School in McKinleyville.

Morris School has a bilingual Spanish-immersion program, and our grandchildren Olivia and Nate have been enrolled in the second- and first-grade classes, respectively, this year. While Sally has been connecting the children in these earlier grades, Rick has been working with fourth-grade teachers and classes. All correspondence has been in Spanish, and there is great enthusiasm for continuing the program during the next school year, when we will be working with second, third, and fifth-grade classes.

During 2009–2010, 180 children participated in the program. Thus, a large number of American and Mexican families have been affected by the correspondence program and hopefully have been gaining a better understanding of one another. Since the letters include content about personal interests, the environment and bird life, community activities, holidays, and other festivities, the children and their families have been exposed to cultural and regional similarities and differences. We have created binders of the children's letters in order to maintain a portfolio of their writings and drawings and to document their accomplishments.

We also developed certificates of participation for all the children, teachers, and administrators involved with the program during the past year. We included colorful maps and photos on the certificates and printed them on heavyweight paper using the color printer in our home.

In addition, we presented educational sets of bilingual books to each classroom to show our appreciation for their participation. We view the project as a very worthy investment!

We sincerely hope that many of the pen-pal amigos will continue their friendships through

Spanish-language correspondence in future years to come. To this end, we plan to provide the necessary support to teachers and children when we return to California at the end of our Peace Corps service in May 2011.

As mentioned in a recent update, we also plan to help launch an Ecoclub with interested middle school and high school youth in the McKinleyville community and to seek out professional colleagues at Humboldt State University who could share their knowledge, skills, and research in relevant social and environmental areas of interest. It would be wonderful, too, if the youth in the McKinleyville Ecoclub could participate in regional events in Spanish-speaking countries and in worldwide conferences as well.

When we sent out the last Sierra Gorda newsletter, HSU colleagues Archie Mossman and Sue Lee noticed the reference to the reserve's First International Forum on Holistic Cattle Ranching. They inquired as to whether the approach was based on Allan Savory's work. Finding out that yes, it is, they put us in direct contact with staff at the Savory Institute. Archie and Sue are longtime friends of Allan and his wife Jody, and this serendipitous link resulted in a possible collaborative connection between the reserve and the Savory Institute. To learn about the amazing work of the Savory Institute, see the website at http://www.savoryinstitute.com/. You may be interested in the accomplishments of its sister organization, the Africa Centre for Holistic Management, which recently won the prestigious Buckminster Fuller award. We appreciate Archie and Sue following up and providing a direct connection with Allan Savory's work since it is pertinent to what the reserve is doing.

Both of us are very grateful for the experiences we've had as Peace Corps volunteers here in the Sierra Gorda. We have learned so much! However, it has become increasingly clear that Rick's professional background is not a good match with the reserve's current programs.

So after some discussion with the reserve's director and with our Peace Corps Mexico environment program manager, it was decided that Sally will continue her affiliation with the reserve, and Rick will explore connections with universities and other organizations that might have projects that could more likely benefit from his expertise. Although Rick has concluded his formal work with the reserve, he will continue to maintain his contacts among the staff and to provide support in every way possible.

We sincerely hope that each of you is doing well. Please drop us a line and fill us in on your latest news. We love hearing from you!

Con cariño,
Rick y Sally

# *Update 23*

## August 2010

¡Hola, familia y amigos!

We hope you enjoyed reading the English version of the July 2010 newsletter from the Alliance for the Conservation of the Sierra Gorda Biosphere Reserve, Querétaro.

Recently, we completed one important phase of our work with the leader of Sierra Gorda Ecotours, Margarita Pedraza Muñoz, in developing itineraries for two programs: an eight-day ecotourism program for international English-speaking tourists, titled "Sustainable Development with a 'Conservation Economy' in the Sierra Gorda," and a three-week course we are proposing to co-facilitate in July 2011 through Humboldt State University's international Sierra Institute, titled "Sustainability in the Sierra Gorda Biosphere." If the course is approved, we would return to Mexico to teach it following our period of Peace Corps service, which ends in May 2011.

Both the proposed ecotourism program and the course include trips for participants to Xilitla (pronounced *hee-léet-la*), which is located in the neighboring state of San Luis Potosí, about two hours northeast of Jalpan and close to La Trinidad, an ecotourism project site at elevations known for their cloud-forest vegetation and diversity of distinctive endemic flora and fauna. Nature tourists find this habitat stunningly beautiful. La Trinidad is one of several ecotourism projects described on the Sierra Gorda website.

Xilitla also is well-known for Las Pozas ("the pools"), a surrealistic sculpture garden in a lush tropical rainforest habitat with myriad waterfalls, cascades, and natural pools. Alongside the garden trails that lead visitors to each sculpture, one can breathe in the sweet fragrance of the lovely, creamy-white mariposa (butterfly) wildflowers.

The garden was designed and developed between 1949 and 1984 by the Scottish poet and artist Edward James. Wikipedia has a brief but fascinating history under the Las Pozas section at http://en.wikipedia.org/wiki/Edward_James. We thoroughly enjoyed meandering about Las Pozas, and we took numerous photos from a variety of vantage points. At the beginning of our tour, we decided to climb the "Fantastic Staircase" to the top, which gave us both a thrill and the heebie-jeebies since there are no handrails and it is, as they say, a very long way down.

Of course, as Peace Corps volunteers, we are keenly aware of the media coverage in the United States regarding safety issues in Mexico. However, we want all of our family and friends to know that the Peace Corps places a high priority on safety for its volunteers in countries throughout the world. And we volunteers are well informed about good safety practices and protocols.

Here in Mexico, for example, volunteers are prohibited from traveling to certain sectors of the country (mostly states on the borders) where violence related to drug cartel activity is occurring (based on the insatiable drug market in the United States). Our Peace Corps Mexico safety and security officer, Malena Vasquez, and PCM country director, Daniel Evans, are continuously in touch with the American embassy and routinely monitor the safety of the areas in which PCM volunteers are serving.

All this is to say that the state of Querétaro (where Peace Corps Mexico headquarters and the Sierra Gorda Biosphere Reserve both are located) is one among many states and regions of Mexico that are viewed as safe for Peace Corps volunteers. The city of Querétaro is known particularly for its tranquility, along with the richness of its cultural history. It also is a very beautiful city.

The two of us firmly believe that ecotourists coming to the Sierra Gorda would gain enormously from a visit to Querétaro and to the reserve. In essence, the Sierra Gorda is a UNESCO World Heritage biosphere reserve and is a world-renowned natural protected area based on its authentic approach to sustainable development with a conservation economy. This approach is radically improving both the environment and the lives of the people who live here. We believe that today's ecotourists need and want to learn about this "green jewel" of Mexico.

Over the past twenty-three years, the Sierra Gorda Ecological Group and Director Pati Ruíz Corzo have received prestigious recognitions along with millions of dollars in funding from diverse national and international agencies and philanthropic organizations in support of their vision, mission, and remarkable accomplishments. Their history of achievements is noteworthy. We sincerely hope that the Sierra Gorda ecotourism proposal will be seen as an appealing opportunity for international travelers in the very near future—and for years to come.

And to any of you who might want to visit us here in Jalpan de Serra between now and May 2011, we welcome you with open arms! *¡Bienvenidos a todos!*

Con cariño,
Rick y Sally

## My PCM Trimester Report
## September 2010

The following is the Peace Corps Mexico (PCM) report I filed with the PCM office in Querétaro in September 2010. The report is organized in the format required. Much of this information is included in preceding and subsequent updates.

### Successes

I am happy to report that the proposed three-week course "Sustainability in the Sierra Gorda Biosphere" that Rick and I submitted to the Humboldt State University (HSU) Extended Education Sierra Institute program has tentatively been approved to offer in July 2011. We are very excited, and we hope that many students will enroll in the course this coming summer!

The chair of the Department of Environmental Science and Management, Dr. Steven Martin, signed his approval of the course on August 20, and Steve wrote that the ENVS 480 course "looks amazing." The course also was approved for 4 units of university credit by the dean's office in the College of Natural Resources and Sciences at HSU. Steve has encouraged the faculty in the department and college to promote the course among their students, and he has suggested to them that the course could be used to fulfill requirements in students' major.

Interestingly, the ENVS department's environmental science degree is focused on "restoring ecosystems, addressing energy and climate issues, and creating policies to solve environmental problems today and for the future." Its environmental management and protection (EMP) degree "is designed to give [students] the skills necessary to understand and manage the ever-changing relationship between humans and the natural world." So the three-week course here in the Sierra Gorda is a very good fit for this department. See http://www.humboldt.edu/environment/envs.html.

The department also provides students with "the opportunity to apply their knowledge to real-world issues such as waste reduction, energy efficiency, and encouraging environmentally sound practices on campus and in the community. Many students in the major participate with the Campus Center for Appropriate Technology (CCAT) and the Green Campus program"—both well-respected HSU student/faculty initiatives.

The Sierra Institute website now has a brief description of the three-week ENVS 480 Sustainability in the Sierra Gorda Biosphere course, listing it as one of the programs for summer 2011. Ward Angles, who is the special projects coordinator for the HSU Office of Extended Education, told us that the course soon will be "activated" on the Sierra Institute website.

In a recent e-mail message, Ward mentioned that he thinks the PowerPoint presentation we submitted based on the Sierra Gorda Ecotours itinerary that Margarita Pedraza Muñoz and her assistant Juan Manuel helped us develop for the course, with the approval of general director Pati Ruíz Corzo, is "superb." Ward also commented that this "is an outstanding program, an *amazing* opportunity for students!" He certainly has been a strong source of support in working with us to meet all the requirements of the department, college, university, and international program committee.

I would be happy to provide the final form that was submitted to HSU's international program committee along with the pre-orientation syllabus intended for students who enroll in the class for Peace Corps Mexico's collection of example programs. I also could send copies of all the other course-related documents, including the most recent copy of the syllabus, course reading list, etc.

Rick and I sincerely appreciate the ongoing interest and support of Margarita Pedraza Muñoz and Pati Ruíz Corzo over these past several months in the process of designing the three-week course. Their assistance in developing the Sierra Gorda Ecotours itinerary was an essential part in the successful completion of the course development. Hopefully, this course will heighten the awareness of many international students about this "green jewel" in the heart of Mexico!

To support my effectiveness in working with the Sierra Gorda Ecotours program, I enrolled in Humboldt State University's online Ecotourism Certificate Program, which includes three courses (http://www.humboldt.edu/ecotour/). The first course began at the end of August, and I have been learning a lot and enjoying it greatly. The text for the course is appropriately titled *Ecotourism and Sustainable Development: Who Owns Paradise?* It was written by Martha Honey (Island Press, 2008) and is an excellent book. I am tailoring all the assignments in the course to the Sierra Gorda context in order to maximize the benefits to the reserve's programs.

In addition to regular Spanish–English translation work, I also am continuing English classes for interested Sierra Gorda staff. In November, I will be working with four people who want to prepare to take the TOEFL examination, which qualifies international students who wish to attend universities in English-language countries around the world. I have enjoyed the opportunity to become better acquainted with the staff and to encourage and support them in improving their confidence and skills. It's very satisfying!

## Challenges

There is one final step in the program approval process for the three-week course I hope to be co-facilitating with Rick here in the Sierra Gorda in July 2011. Apparently, the California State University chancellor's office will not be approving study programs involving Mexico until early 2011. However, HSU extended education special programs coordinator Ward Angles told us that the Sierra Institute is permitted to advertise the program in the meantime, as long as we include a disclaimer, "subject to approval by the CSU chancellor's office" or something similar. Hopefully, the course will be given chancellor's office approval in January.

The current reality is that the State Department changed its travel advisory for Mexico on September 10, 2010. Rick and I carefully reviewed the advisory, and we shared the information with colleagues in Sierra Gorda and Peace Corps Mexico as well as with Steve Martin, so he is well informed about the current situation. We prefer to inform everyone who needs to know about the advisory without sensationalizing the negative aspects.

In fact, as part of the information submitted to the HSU international program committee concerning the political climate here in Mexico (which also is being reviewed by the CSU chancellor's office), we wrote:

As Peace Corps volunteers, we are keenly aware of the media coverage in the U.S. regarding safety issues in Mexico. However, it is helpful to know that the Peace Corps places a high priority on safety for its volunteers in countries throughout the world. And we volunteers are well informed about good safety practices and protocols.

Here in Mexico, volunteers are prohibited from traveling to certain sectors of the country (mostly states on the borders) where violence related to drug cartel activity is occurring (based on the insatiable drug market in the U.S.). Our Peace Corps Mexico safety and security officer, Malena Vasquez, and PCM country director, Daniel Evans, are continuously in touch with the American Embassy and routinely monitoring the safety of the areas in which PCM volunteers are serving. (Dan Evans: devans@mx.peacecorps.gov)

The state of Querétaro (where Peace Corps Mexico headquarters and the Sierra Gorda Biosphere Reserve both are located) is one among many states and regions of Mexico that are viewed as safe for Peace Corps volunteers. The city of Querétaro is known particularly for its tranquility, along with the richness of its cultural history. It also is a very beautiful city.

The faculty members firmly believe that ecotourists and university students coming to the Sierra Gorda would gain enormously from a visit to Querétaro and to the reserve. In essence, the Sierra Gorda is a UNESCO World Heritage biosphere reserve and is a world-renowned natural protected area based on its authentic approach to sustainable development with a "conservation economy." This approach is radically improving both the environment and the lives of the people who live here. We believe that today's ecotourists and students need and want to learn about this "green jewel" of Mexico.

### Lessons Learned

One of the most significant lessons I have learned over the course of my Peace Corps Mexico service is that "life goes on" and "this too shall pass." I have become more keenly aware of my own finitude and vulnerability and more appreciative of my strong family relationships. Rick and I feel incredibly fortunate to have one another's friendship and support, and our relationship has deepened during this period of Peace Corps service.

We both have missed our family and friends a great deal. However, by being away from all of them, we have become even closer to one another. This has been especially important during times of loss. A dear friend died last March, and we mourned his death together—both having known and loved him greatly.

In July, our brother-in-law suffered a heart attack and then had a successful bypass surgery. Both Rick and I were able to extend support to my sister and her family, albeit through phone calls and Skype conversations. Skype has been such a blessing for us in that we can see our dear ones and communicate with them on a regular basis—usually on Sunday afternoons. Last Sunday, our grandson Nate read us a Spanish-language book from his second-grade class. He took such pleasure in sharing his skills, and Rick and I felt reaffirmed in our own strong commitment to increasing our fluency in Spanish.

Rick will be 69 in January, and next month I will be 68—the same age as Lillian Gorda Carter when she began her own service as a Peace Corps volunteer in India. As a retired nurse, following her three-month period of preservice training, Lillian Carter worked for nearly two years at the Godrej Colony near Mumbai, where she assisted patients, including some with leprosy.

As a Peace Corps Mexico volunteer serving at nearly the same age as was Lillian Gordy Carter, I hope to inspire other retirees to consider Peace Corps service. While volunteers seek to fulfill the primary goal of sharing knowledge and skills in countries that welcome their contributions, they also seek to improve understanding between the people in those countries and people in the United States. The so-called second and third goals of Peace Corps service are, in my mind, equally as important as the first goal. This too is one of the most valuable lessons I have learned.

Returned volunteers who have served over the years in countries around the world will be joining Peace Corps director Aaron Williams for the 50th anniversary of Peace Corps in September 2011 in Washington, D.C. We'll be there!

## Activities

During this trimester, I completed 39 translations of documents that included proposals, reports, agendas of courses and workshops, descriptions for the Sierra Gorda website, monthly newsletters, professional correspondence, etc. Most of the translations were from Spanish to English; however, a few of the longer reports were from English to Spanish.

During this trimester, I taught 37 English-language classes for Sierra Gorda staff and colleagues. Beginning in September, I added a second basic-level class. In November, I will be helping prepare four staff to take the TOEFL exam so that they can meet eligibility requirements for admission to universities in which English is the language of instruction. One of these staff plans to attend a university in Costa Rica that offers doctoral degrees related to his professional interests in forestry and reforestation.

## Goals Two and Three

### Americans

Whenever Rick and I send our monthly updates to family and friends about our experience as Peace Corps Mexico volunteers, we include the link to the English version of the current monthly newsletter of the Alliance for the Conservation of the Sierra Gorda Biosphere Reserve, Querétaro. This provides valuable information that highlights the fine work being accomplished here while helping to educate people in the United States about Mexico.

In July, we completed an important phase of our work with the leader of Sierra Gorda Ecotours, Margarita Pedraza Muñoz, in developing itineraries for two programs: an eight-day ecotourism program for international English-speaking tourists, titled "Sustainable Development with a 'Conservation Economy' in the Sierra Gorda," and a three-week course we are proposing to co-facilitate in July 2011 through Humboldt State University's international Sierra Institute, titled "Sustainability in the Sierra Gorda Biosphere." If the course is approved, we would return to Mexico to teach it following our period of Peace Corps service, which ends in May 2011.

In our updates, we emphasize that over the past 23 years the Sierra Gorda Ecological Group and Director Pati Ruíz Corzo have received prestigious recognitions along with millions of dollars in funding from diverse national and international agencies and philanthropic organizations in support of their vision, mission, and remarkable accomplishments. Their history of achievements is noteworthy. We also emphasize that we hope the Sierra Gorda ecotourism proposal will be seen as an appealing opportunity for international travelers in the very near future—and for years to come. We have extended personal invitations to family and friends to visit us here in Jalpan before the end of our PCM service in May 2011.

In a recent update, we explained that Mexico was preparing for festivities to celebrate the bicentennial commemoration of the country's independence from Spain on September 16, and we provided a Wikipedia article with several good links to help family and friends explore some basic information about Mexico's history. We enjoyed attending the bicentennial events in Querétaro and will be sharing photos and summaries of our experiences in our October update.

In June, Rick and I were very excited that a number of our children and grandchildren were able to join us for a week of vacation here in Mexico. They flew into Guadalajara, and we traveled from there to Lake Chapala—Mexico's largest natural lake—and to Zacatecas, a center of historical and cultural significance. It was so much fun to be together! For most of our children and grandchildren, this was their first experience of traveling in Mexico, and we could see how much they were learning during the guided tours we took and our visits to cultural and historical sites, including traditional *mercados*. Olivia and Nate enjoyed practicing their Spanish with local people, and their parents, aunts, uncle, and cousins were quite impressed—as were we!

## Mexicans

Rick and I recently completed the process of getting organized to continue the pen-pal exchange program for 2010–2011. Early in September, we met with the directors and teachers for the second, third, and fifth graders at the Benito Juárez and Melchor Ocampo primary schools here in Jalpan. We also reconnected with the principal and teachers at Morris School in McKinleyville, CA, where two of our grandchildren (third grader Olivia and second grader Nate) are enrolled in the Spanish-immersion program.

At the schools here, we took new photos of all the kids to send to their pen pals with their first letters for fall 2010. The children have grown so much over the summer! It is wonderful to have the young students recognize and greet us when we are out and about in town. It really gives my heart a lift when the younger ones see me on the street and call out, "¡Hola, Maestra!"

Rick and I are impressed with the Ecoclubs of the Sierra Gorda and their support of youth leadership development in promoting all aspects of school and community environmental responsibility. When we return to California, we plan to explore the possibility of establishing an Ecoclub for youth in our area. (At this time, there are no Ecoclubs in the U.S.) One day, we would love to accompany a group from Northern California to a regional Ecoclub meeting here in Mexico and witness the first face-to-face meetings of some of the pen pals. That would be a joy!

During the summer, we were invited to attend the Quinceañera of the sister of a participant in one of my English classes. It was an opportunity to experience a unique celebration that not every 15-year-old girl is privileged to enjoy. To date, Rick and/or I have attended a few birthday parties and many religious or traditional celebrations, including baby showers, a baptism, a funeral, the Día de los Muertos, and the Quinceañera. We have not been invited to a wedding yet, but we hope we will be before too long!

In all of these activities, Rick and I are able to serve as models of "typical Americans" and share our experiences and impressions with our new colleagues and friends. As I have mentioned in other reports, we enjoy making connections and having conversations in many different social contexts.

# Update 24

## September 2010

¡Hola, familia y amigos!

The English version of the current monthly newsletter, "Viva la Patria—Celebrate Mexico," from the Alliance for the Conservation of the Sierra Gorda Biosphere Reserve, Querétaro, can be accessed online. The photo of the month features a darling little Sierra Gorda tree frog. It's sweet!

Here in Mexico right now, people throughout the entire country are preparing for festivities to celebrate the upcoming bicentennial commemoration on September 16. A Wikipedia article with several good links you may find interesting has basic information about Mexico's history and can be found at http://en.wikipedia.org/wiki/Grito_de_Dolores.

Although many folks will be traveling to Mexico City to gather at midnight on September 15 for the country's best-attended "Grito de la Independencia" ("Cry of Independence"), the two of us have decided to stay here in Jalpan de Serra and observe the holiday as it is honored by the many local schoolchildren, families, dignitaries, and other community members. This will be another great photo opportunity!*

We are in the process of getting organized to continue the pen-pal exchange program for 2010–2011. Earlier this week, we met with the directors and teachers for the second, third, and fifth graders at the Benito Juárez and Melchor Ocampo primary schools. We also are connecting with the principal and teachers at Morris School in McKinleyville, California, where—as you may recall—two of our grandchildren (third grader Olivia and second grader Nate) are enrolled in the Spanish-immersion program.

Next week, we will be taking photos of all the kids at the schools here to send to their pen pals with their first letters for fall 2010. The children have grown so much over the summer! It is wonderful to have the young students recognize and greet us when we are out and about in town. It really gives Sally's heart a lift when the younger ones see her on the street and call out, "¡Hola, Maestra!"

To support her effectiveness in working with the Sierra Gorda Ecotours program, Sally enrolled in Humboldt State University's online Ecotourism Certificate Program, which includes three courses (http://www.humboldt.edu/ecotour/). The first course just began last week, and Sally is learning a lot and enjoying it greatly. The text for the course is appropriately titled *Ecotourism and Sustainable Development: Who Owns Paradise?* It is written by Martha Honey (Island Press, 2008) and is an excellent book. Sally is tailoring all the assignments in the course to the Sierra Gorda context in order to maximize the benefits to the reserve's programs.

In addition to regular Spanish–English translation work, Sally also is continuing English classes for interested Sierra Gorda staff. In November, she will be working with just a few people who want to prepare to take the TOEFL examination, which qualifies international students who wish to attend universities in English-language countries around the world. Sally has enjoyed the opportunity to become better acquainted with the staff and to encourage and support them in improving their confidence and skills. It's very satisfying!

Rick's work has broadened. He has forged a good connection with the Office of Tourism in the municipality of Pinal de Amoles, where he is facilitating English classes for staff members and helping them develop English-language brochures to distribute to international tourists visiting the distinctive regional communities they represent.

In addition, Rick is working with the young tour guides in one of the Pinal area's most beautiful ecotourism destinations, Cuatro Palos. Here, too, he is teaching English classes with lessons that include content about the natural history and ecology of the region and translations of key vocabulary. As part of a Peace Corps grant focused on science education, Rick was able to purchase and distribute Spanish–English pocket dictionaries for the young guides, and they were quite pleased to get them. The dictionaries will allow the youth to be more independent learners and also will support them as they progress in their future academic and career goals.

Rick also serves as a volunteer every Wednesday at the Vicente Guerrero School, a small, rural school with two multi-grade classrooms located in the community of San Vicente within the municipality of Jalpan de Serra. Rick first met the school's new director, Professor Ángel García, at the Benito Juárez primary school last year when they collaborated on the pen-pal exchange program.

When Professor García told Rick he was going to be relocating, the two men agreed they would continue their collaboration at the new school. Professor García asked Rick to assume some teaching responsibilities with both the younger and the older classes. For each group, Rick teaches classes in English, science education, and ecology. Rick also is helping the community of San Vicente improve its recycling programs, and he currently is trying to connect Sierra Gorda environmental education staff with community leaders there.

Based on his past experiences in academe, Rick also has been appointed formally to work as a Peace Corps volunteer at the Jalpan campus of the Universidad Tecnológica de San Juan del Río. This semester, he has been assigned four classes per week in which he guides and facilitates English-language discussions on professionally related topics: two classes of ecotourism students and two of business development students.

Rick also will be mentoring at least one young professor on strategies for developing a research agenda, conducting research, working on research projects with students, and writing for professional publication. He is continuing to collaborate with faculty at the Universidad Nacional Autónoma Mexico in Mexico City regarding amphibian diseases.

As you can see, we both are keeping pretty busy as Peace Corps volunteers here in Mexico. We know that you also have busy lives, and we appreciate the time you take to allow us to share our experiences with you. ¡Muchas gracias! When you have a moment, please share some highlights of your own recent experiences. We love hearing from family and friends!

We hope that all of you are doing well and that you are finding the changing seasons and back-to-school activities enjoyable. As Labor Day approaches in the United States, we are sending wishes for a very safe and pleasant holiday.

Con cariño,
Rick y Sally

*Postscript: After deciding to stay in Jalpan for Mexico's exciting September 2010 bicentennial events, the two of us traveled to the city of Querétaro to help celebrate this historic occasion there. We also enjoyed the farewell party in honor of Peace Corps Mexico's outgoing country director Byron Battle and his wife Margarita. Byron is now the PCM country director emeritus, supporting the transition for Dan and Julia Evans. Byron's party and the 2010 bicentennial events both in Querétaro and in Jalpan were lots of fun!

Mexico's bicentenary, 1810–2010.

# Update 25

## October 2010

¡Hola, familia y amigos!

The English version of the current newsletter of the Alliance for the Conservation of the Sierra Gorda is available now. There are several excellent links within the newsletter connecting to photographs and videos that graphically portray the inexpressible beauty of the Sierra Gorda Biosphere region of Querétaro as well as the important work being accomplished here in sustainable development with a conservation economy and in well-coordinated activities to confront global climate change (we'll be attending the 10/10/10 event). We are pleased that the newsletter features an article about the Savory Institute, which now is collaborating with Sierra Gorda. Again, thanks to Rick's colleagues Archie Mossman and Sue Lee for helping make the connection with Allan Savory's work in holistic management a few months ago.

Since the two of us are now both sixty-eight, we want to acknowledge the inspiration of Lillian Gordy Carter. She was a person of great integrity with a deep commitment to social justice, activism, and community and international service. As a retired nurse, following her three-month period of preservice training, Lillian Carter worked for nearly two years at the Godrej Colony near Mumbai, where she assisted patients, including some with leprosy.

As Peace Corps Mexico volunteers serving at nearly the same age as was Lillian Gordy Carter, we encourage other retirees to consider Peace Corps service. Although volunteers seek to fulfill the primary goal of sharing knowledge and skills in countries that welcome their contributions, they also seek to improve understanding between the people in those countries and people in the United States. The so-called second and third goals of Peace Corps service are, in our minds, equally as important as the first goal.

We are happy to report that the proposed three-week course "Sustainability in the Sierra Gorda Biosphere" that we submitted to the Humboldt State University (HSU) Extended Education Sierra Institute program has tentatively been approved, to be offered in July 2011. The course focuses on the distinctive approach to sustainable development with the "conservation economy" of the Sierra Gorda, and we hope that many students will enroll in the course this coming summer.

The Sierra Institute website now has a description of the course, listing it as one of the programs for summer 2011. Ward Angles, who is the special projects coordinator for the HSU Office of Extended Education, commented that this "is an outstanding program, an *amazing* opportunity for students!" He certainly has been a strong source of support in working with us to meet all the requirements of the department, college, university, and international program committee.

Rick and I sincerely appreciate the ongoing interest and support of Margarita Pedraza Muñoz and Pati Ruíz Corzo over these past several months in the process of designing the three-week course. Their assistance in developing the Sierra Gorda Ecotours itinerary was an essential part in the successful completion of the course development. Hopefully, this course will heighten the awareness of many international students about this "green jewel" in the heart of Mexico!

There is one final step in the program approval process for the three-week course since the California State University chancellor's office will not be approving study programs involving Mexico until early 2011. However, Ward told us that the Sierra Institute is permitted to advertise the program in the meantime, as long as it includes a disclaimer such as "subject to approval by the CSU chancellor's office." Hopefully, the course will be given chancellor's office approval in January.

We truly hope you are enjoying the changing seasons and the beauty of colorful autumn vistas. Please let us know how things are going in your neck of the woods!

Con cariño,
Rick y Sally

### Additional Message Later in October

¡Hola, familia y amigos!

The current newsletter of the Alliance for the Conservation of the Sierra Gorda is at http://www.sierragorda.net/noticias/bol10j-.htm [link no longer active]. We invite you all to join us in voting for the Sierra Gorda "Value of Nature" project. The deadline for voting is October 31. Hope you all are doing very well!

Con cariño,
Rick y Sally

# *Update 26*

## November 2010

El 25 de Noviembre 2010
¡Feliz Día de la Acción de Gracias! Happy Thanksgiving Day!
¡Muchas gracias! Many thanks!

¡Les agradecemos por tener su presencia en nuestras vidas! We are
grateful for having you in our lives!

Con cariño,
Rick y Sally

# Update 27

## December 3, 2010

¡Hola, familia y amigos!

It is hard for us to believe that we have been living and working as Peace Corps Mexico volunteers here in the Sierra Gorda for over eighteen months. With less than six months until we return home to California in May 2011, we continue to feel very grateful for this rich international service opportunity.

Along with PCM country director Dan Evans and his lovely wife Julia Tully, we co-hosted an early evening Thanksgiving Day celebration with colleagues at the Sierra Gorda Earth Center facility. Dan and Julia brought the turkey, which we roasted during the afternoon in the just-big-enough oven that the Peace Corps had issued us.

Side dishes were catered by a local family business, and the tables in the Sierra Gorda *palapas* were decorated with handmade ceramic candleholders with tall, gold candles—a lovely sight. Dan spoke a few words of appreciation for the Sierra Gorda/Peace Corps connection, and we all enjoyed el Día de la Acción de Gracias together. Dan also visited Rick's class at the university and discussed the work there with Rick's colleagues and students.

During their Thanksgiving visit, Dan and Julia also took us to Xilitla for another visit to Las Pozas—the sculpture garden created by Scottish artist Edward James. It was kind of Dan and Julia to take us to Xilitla and great fun to tour this amazing living exhibit again!

The two of us are thrilled that our son Tin will be able to join us for Christmas here in Mexico. Tin wasn't able to join us for the family vacation in Guadalajara last June; he was in the midst of relocating from New York to California in order to complete his specialization in cardiology through the University of Southern California. It is wonderful that he will be able to come down from Los Angeles for a Christmas visit. We also plan to connect with our other children and the grandchildren via Skype on Christmas Day. That should be lots of fun!

Both of us are keeping quite busy with all our projects. It will be nice to have some vacation time for the holidays and to get revitalized for the homestretch. We hope that each and every one of you is doing well and that your preparations for the coming holidays are as relaxed and enjoyable as possible!

Con cariño,
Rick y Sally

# *Update 28*

## December 15, 2010

Dear family and friends:

¡Feliz Navidad! Merry Christmas! ¡Feliz Año Nuevo! Happy New Year! Our warmest wishes to all of you for safe and joyful holidays wherever you may be celebrating them.

We will be here in Jalpan de Serra for our last Christmas as Peace Corps volunteers, and we are looking forward to having our son Tin here with us. We also will be enjoying Skype visits with our other children and grandchildren on Christmas Day.

On Christmas Eve, we'll attend the evening mass at Jalpan's historic mission, which is located only a couple of blocks from our home. Just across from the mission, the town's main garden plaza has been decorated with a community Christmas tree, a large nativity scene, and hundreds of bright red and green poinsettias—known as the "Flor de la Nochebuena" (Christmas Eve flower).

As mentioned in a previous update, Jalpan de Serra was selected as Mexico's thirty-seventh "magical village" on October 19. The Sierra Gorda Biosphere Reserve celebrated along with the people of Jalpan since renewed interest in Jalpan certainly will enhance interest in the work of the reserve and in its many appealing ecotourism destinations. Of course, the underlying motivation for the reserve is to promote sustainable development with a conservation economy that benefits both the environment and the people who live here.

In an effort to get the word out about the connection between the various sources of local and regional pride, the Alliance for the Conservation of the Sierra Gorda published an article highlighting the five Franciscan missions in the region, which are promoted for the cultural heritage they represent. The article showcased the reserve within the context of the region's cultural significance and capitalized on an opportunity to promote the Sierra Gorda vision. It invited those visiting the five missions to add a reserve destination to their itinerary—an invitation we hope many will accept.

Again, we wish you the happiest of holidays!

Con cariño,
Rick y Sally

# *Update 29*

## December 18, 2010—Sierra Gorda End-of-Year Appeal
## Sierra Gorda End-of-Year Fundraising
## Appeal from Sally Botzler, PCM
## English Version

December 18, 2010

Dear Friend of the Sierra Gorda:

As a supporter of the Sierra Gorda Biosphere Reserve in Querétaro, Mexico, I am writing to invite you to make a special year-end contribution.

There are 30 women in the community of La Colgada who are operating a very successful micro-enterprise in embroidery products; yet the building they own as headquarters was poorly constructed, and it is expensive to repair the roof of the building.

Each rain puts their raw materials and products in peril. This small business is providing rural women hope, support, and an increasingly sustainable livelihood for their families through their social enterprise of handmade, traditional-style embroideries that incorporate nature motifs.

Following heavy rainfalls this year, the roof of the building where the women work was damaged badly. The amount needed to complete the roof repair is US$3,500. For the last five years they have worked hard, and success has led to the first sales to an international market—an expensive learning process. Therefore, the cost to repair the roof is beyond their ability to pay.

I first traveled to La Colgada to observe the embroidery workshop in May 2009, shortly after arriving in the Sierra Gorda with my husband Rick as Peace Corps Mexico volunteers. It was inspiring for me to meet the women, tour the building, and witness the strong support provided for the micro-enterprise by Sierra Gorda products and services staff and consultant Dorothy Yuki, who regularly comes to La Colgada from the San Francisco Bay Area in California to teach new stitching, fabric preparation, and assembly techniques.

The day I visited, a young girl was concentrating on a piece of nature embroidery while lovingly supporting her baby sister on her lap. I asked their mother if I could take a picture, and she gave me permission to share the photo. Developing a sustainable business in this remote community strengthens the role of women in local economies and provides a better future for the families in La Colgada.

When Rick and I learned about the damaged roof and the US$3,500 needed to repair it, we decided not only to make a contribution ourselves but to appeal to others who might also have the means to assist with this special project. Please join us by making a year-end contribution to the <u>Women & Nature Fund.</u> Whatever you are able to contribute will be truly appreciated by the women in the La Colgada embroidery cooperative and their families.

You can make a tax-deductible contribution to the non-profit Earth Island Institute's Women & Nature Fund. On the donor page, simply write "La Colgada" or "Women & Nature" in the Comments box.

If you would like more information, please contact me at <u>botzlers@sbcglobal.net</u>, and I will share your request with Laura Pérez-Arce, director of Viva Sierra Gorda.

Thank you for considering this invitation and for forwarding it to your friends!

Sincerely,
Sally Botzler
Peace Corps Mexico volunteer, Sierra Gorda Biosphere Reserve, Querétaro

### Versión Española de Sally Botzler, PCM
### Cooperativa Rural: *"Bordados hechos a mano con motivos de la naturaleza"*

18 Diciembre 2010

Querido Amigo de Sierra Gorda:

Como donante de la Reserva de la Biosfera Sierra Gorda ubicada en Querétaro, México, te escribo para invitarte a realizar una contribución muy especial para este fin de año.

En la comunidad de La Colgada hay treinta mujeres que les operan una empresa muy exitosa en productos de bordado; sin embargo, la construcción del taller donde realizan sus actividades fue mal realizada y cuesta mucho reparar el techo.

Tal situación y con cada lluvia se pone en riesgo sus materias primas y el producto que realizan con tanta dedicación. Para estas mujeres rurales, la pequeña empresa donde realizan a mano bordados de estilo tradicional con motivos de naturaleza, les proporciona esperanza, apoyo, y un sustento cada vez más sostenible para sus familias.

Este año, después de las fuertes lluvias registradas el techo del taller donde trabajan resultó gravemente dañado y la cantidad necesaria para completar la reparación es de 43,500 pesos. Desde hace cinco años ellas han trabajado arduamente y su éxito las ha llevado a sus primeras ventas a un mercado internacional, que resultó en un proceso caro de aprendizaje. Por lo tanto, el costo para reparar el techo está más allá de sus recursos y posibilidades.

La primera vez que viajé a La Colgada para ver el taller de bordado fue poco después de haber llegado a Sierra Gorda con mi esposo Rick como voluntarios del Cuerpo de Paz México en mayo de 2009. Para mí, fue realmente inspirador conocer a estas mujeres, dar un tour por el taller y presenciar el fuerte apoyo que Productos y Servicios Sierra Gorda provee a esta microempresa a través de Dorothy Yuki, una consultora y voluntaria que viaja regularmente a La Colgada. Dorothy viene de la Bahía de San Francisco en California, EUA, para enseñarles nuevas costuras, la preparación del tejido y técnicas de ensamblaje.

Aquel día que estuve de visita, una joven chica se concentraba en una pieza de bordado de naturaleza mientras que sostenía con cariño en su regazo a su hermana de tan solo unos meses de edad; le pregunté a la madre si podría tomar una imagen y si me daría su permiso para compartir la foto.

Desarrollar un negocio sostenible en esta comunidad remota sin duda refuerza el rol de las mujeres en las economías locales y proporciona un mejor futuro para las familias en La Colgada.

## Women and Nature

Haz un regalo en estas fiestas al fondo para las Mujeres & Naturaleza, tu participación cuenta. Esta campaña de recaudación es limitada a diciembre, compártela con tus amigos.

Give a gift this season to the Women & Nature Fund. Thanks for your support. This fundraising campaign is limited to December 2010. Please share it with your friends.

# *Update 30*

## February 11, 2011
## Our Last One Hundred Days as Peace Corps Mexico Volunteers

¡Hola, familia y amigos!

As we begin our last one hundred days as Peace Corps Mexico volunteers and start preparing to return home to California—around May 23—we wish you all a ¡Feliz Día del Amor y de la Amistad! Here in Mexico, St. Valentine's Day is known as "the day of love and friendship." Since one of Peace Corps' primary goals is to build peace and friendship between people in the United States and its host countries, we truly are celebrating the fiftieth anniversary of Peace Corps with great joy. We know the friendships we have developed here in Mexico will last for the rest of our lives. We hope to return often to Mexico as well as to host many of our newfound Mexican friends in our California home after our return.

As you know, one of the key projects on which we have been collaborating is the development of a university connection with the Sierra Gorda. We created a three-week course for English-speaking university students. The course was approved by the chair of the Department of Environmental Science and Management at Humboldt State University in Northern California, and we hope to co-facilitate the course here in the Sierra Gorda in July 2011. The course focuses on the successful ongoing sustainable development strategies implemented for over twenty-two years in the Sierra Gorda Biosphere Reserve—strategies that are distinctive in their emphasis on establishing a conservation economy that benefits the well-being both of the environment in this natural protected area and of the people living here.

Our challenge at the moment is that, due to concerns about safety issues, all international study programs in Mexico to be offered through any of the twenty-three campuses in the California State University system now require the formal approval of the campus president (in this case, HSU president Rollin C. Richmond) as well as the CSU chancellor, Charles B. Reed. Thus, we have solicited letters of assurance about safety in the state of Querétaro from Peace Corps Mexico country director Daniel Evans and the general director of the Alliance for the Conservation of the Sierra Gorda, Martha Isabel "Pati" Ruíz Corzo. We hope that President Richmond and Chancellor Reed will find the letters of assurance sufficient for approving the July 2011 course.

A second challenge we have faced is related to the pen-pal correspondence program we created between three grade levels of students at two elementary schools here in Jalpan de Serra and the corresponding grade-level classes at the bilingual Spanish-immersion elementary school in our home community in Northern California, where two of our grandchildren attend. Last year, the letter exchange was fairly frequent.

For some reason, this year the postal service between Mexico and the United States has been very slow, and one packet of letter templates was never even delivered. (Similarly, Sally's sister Cindy sent a box of candies and cookies for Christmas on December 7, and it just arrived on February 11—in time for Valentine's Day, though!) The unpredictable quality of postal service has been very frustrating, and it has required extra work on the part of the teachers in California. This has resulted in fewer letter exchanges between the students. We now have decided to avoid using the post offices and instead to use FedEx for sending the packages of letters between the countries.

One important project in which Sally has been engaged is related to ecotourism in the Sierra Gorda. In the process of translating some Sierra Gorda documents last year, Sally learned that the Alliance for the Conservation of the Sierra Gorda had received significant funding from the Inter-American Development Bank and that Sierra Gorda leaders were planning to expand and improve the reserve's ecotourism program because they view it as the culminating sustainable development strategy, with great potential for enhancing the region's conservation economy and benefiting both the environment and its inhabitants. Realizing that she knew very little about ecotourism, Sally decided to become better educated by enrolling in the online Ecotourism Certificate Program (ECP) at HSU.

In collaboration with Sierra Gorda Ecotours coordinator Margarita Pedraza Muñoz, we already had designed an ecotourism itinerary for international visitors focused on the reserve's distinctive approach to sustainable development with a conservation economy. As a student in the ECP, Sally has tailored all of her assignments to the Sierra Gorda Ecotours program and the destinations in its network of eco-lodges.

One of the most important lessons that Sally learned in her first ECP course is that a region can have the most appealing ecotourism destination in the world, but if there is no effort to market the destination to the "niche" of potential visitors, it will not be successful. In general, word-of-mouth advertising is insufficient. Also, nowadays ecotourism destinations are marketed in very sophisticated ways in an increasingly online environment.

Currently, Sally is enrolled in the second ECP course, which focuses primarily on sustainable and responsible ecotourism and on the carbon footprint and carbon offsets that need to be taken into consideration. A wonderful side effect of Sally's participation in the ECP is that she and Rick will be hosting HSU Ecotourism Certificate director Michael Sweeney and his wife Leslie, who will be coming for a "reconnaissance" ecotourism visit to the Sierra Gorda in mid-March. Michael has been invited to meet with general director Pati Ruíz Corzo to discuss state-of-the-art ideas in ecotourism site development that might be helpful to the Sierra Gorda.

In addition to the shared collaboration with Sally for the Sierra Institute course and the pen-pal exchange program, Rick has been active in several areas of concentration. His work in English-as-a-second-language (ESL) classes is the common theme uniting most of these activities.

At the Vicente Guerrero Primary School in the community of San Vicente within the municipality of Jalpan de Serra, Rick has worked under the mentorship of Professor Ángel García, sole teacher and the director of the school. In addition to teaching ESL and science-related lessons to first through third graders on Wednesday mornings and to fourth through sixth graders in the afternoons, Rick has helped connect the San Vicente community with the Sierra Gorda Biosphere Reserve to reestablish a recycling program there, to develop an organic garden at the school as a teaching tool, and to bring environmental education presentations, including an Earth Festival.

In the nearby municipality of Pinal de Amoles, Rick facilitates an ESL class at the Office of Tourism for staff preparing for international tourists. He also has incorporated members from the nearby community of La Quebradora into the class. In the Pinal community of Cuatro Palos, Rick has met with the young guides nearly every Saturday, providing both ESL classes and sessions to increase their knowledge about the ecology of the region and their skills in effectively serving as guides for domestic and international ecotourists.

Rick facilitates four discussion-circle classes for the ninety students enrolled in the Jalpan Academic Unit of the Universidad Tecnológica de San Juan del Río—two classes for students majoring in ecotourism and two for those in the business development program. He also is assisting two of the university professors in preparing research proposals for their doctoral studies. Rick recently was invited to give a workshop on writing and editing scientific articles at the main campus in San Juan del Río.

Also, Rick currently is concluding a research project with Dr. Gabriella Parra Olea at the Universidad Nacional Autónoma de Mexico in Mexico City on a chytrid fungus study. They hope to present some of their results at the Wildlife Disease Association Conference in Quebec City, Canada, in August 2011.

Rick wrote an opinion piece assessing current attitudes toward the use of basic research in natural protected areas in Mexico, with recommendations for stronger research programs in these regions. Recently, the short article was published in *La Piñata*, an in-house Peace Corps Mexico bulletin (see below).

In relation to Peace Corps goals, both of us continue to believe that the pen-pal exchange program is functioning well in promoting a better understanding between Mexicans and Americans. It is particularly meaningful, in our opinion, that the children who are participating are young.

As students in the second, third, and fifth grades, they are very receptive to one another, enthusiastic about the correspondence, eager to sustain the connection, and always excited about getting another letter from their amigos and amigas. It also is significant that the correspondence is completely in Spanish, which allows the children in California to strengthen their Spanish-language skills in the process.

We will continue supporting the pen-pal program when we return home to California, and we are still planning to begin an Ecoclub in our region that has the potential to establish enduring relationships between children, youth, and their families and communities over time while simultaneously developing youth leadership on environmental issues in our community.

Please let us know how you are doing—we really love hearing from family and friends. We hope Valentine's Day 2011 is filled with love, peace, and friendship!

Con cariño,
Rick and Sally

### Article Published in Peace Corps Mexico's *La Piñata* by Rick Botzler
### Basic Scientific Research in Mexico's Natural Protected Areas: A Proposal

After some rich discussions with Peace Corps Mexico volunteers and staff, Mexican university researchers, and personnel in some of Mexico's Natural Protected Areas (NPAs), I now am seeking broader dialogue on an important topic: the potential value for increasing basic scientific research in Mexico's NPAs. I propose that the Commission on Natural Protected Areas (CONANP) actively develop and support management plans for identifying key NPA needs and that it adopt a policy to promote and encourage ongoing basic scientific research programs to address those needs. Such a policy would result in key learning and management tools for increasing the long-term health and well-being of NPA environments in the country.

I received many valuable ideas from the numerous reviewers listed in the Acknowledgment Section. However, the ideas in this proposal are entirely my responsibility and are not intended to reflect official positions of Peace Corps Mexico, CONANP, any NGOs, any group of university personnel, or any other individual. I also take full responsibility for any errors or misrepresentations of their ideas.

As one Mexican researcher reviewing an earlier draft of this article eloquently stated, "No se puede proteger lo que no se conoce" (You cannot protect what you do not know). This proposed change would be a significant shift in CONANP policy, and could require adjustments in funding, agency policies, and political strategies. Current policies in Mexico do not designate CONANP as a research institution; thus, even though CONANP is permitted to use some of its funds for conservation activities, these funds generally are not designated for basic scientific research activities.

Some have found that the central administrative leadership within CONANP usually does not give much support for basic scientific research and may view it as a minor part of the more significant issues the staff faces. One reviewer also noted that a complicating factor is that many of the people assigned to key positions in CONANP have little knowledge or experience in biology or ecology, however are appointed to their positions based on their political profiles and affiliations.

Funding is another concern. Although current funding has been increasing, CONANP's overall funding generally still is quite limited. Consequently, almost all basic scientific research in ANPs is connected to outside work, particularly by university-based scientists who view many of these protected areas as important study sites for their specific research programs.

It appears that past attitudes by some NPA administrators towards the participation of outside researchers have been mixed. In some cases, outside researchers have been welcomed and even encouraged to work in NPAs; commonly, their reception has depended on the research programs being self-sufficient and not requiring significant support from CONANP funds or personnel. In other cases, administrators of NPAs have been less welcoming of basic scientific research and, occasionally, even have prohibited outside researchers from conducting studies on the NPAs. In these latter cases, some science-oriented projects still may be conducted on the NPAs, but these projects commonly involve internal staff or consultants collecting data required for certification/

verification programs, or conducting projects intended to provide relatively quick answers to specific environmental problems of concern to the administrators of the NPAs.

Cases of strong resistance to basic scientific research appear to have a somewhat complex history. For example, in the past, university researchers sometimes have behaved irresponsibly by failing to gain proper permissions and/or authorizations for conducting their research, and/or by leaving evidence of environmental damage related to their activities. In other cases, there have been conflicts between certain universities and NPA program administrators that have provoked visiting researchers to use their scientific findings to directly criticize or undermine the policies of an NPA administrator. One reviewer of an earlier draft noted that university researchers have not always established good relations with NPA administrators or with the local people in their study areas. Nor have they always acknowledged the support they received from these groups.

Some of these past problems probably contributed to the development of national ethical guidelines and laws for conducting basic scientific research on natural protected lands, such as the Ley General De Vida Silvestre (Diario Oficial de la Federación el 3 de Julio de 2000, y de 30 de noviembre de 2006), and others. But even with these guidelines and laws, resistance to outside scientific researchers has lingered in the memories among some NPA administrators.

Another issue that has generated some tensions has been the relatively slow reporting of data and analyses from past university-based research studies to NPA administrators and managers for use in their subsequent policy decisions in the NPAs. And even when research results have been provided, they often were copies of technical papers in which the specialized language was not readily accessible to the local peoples who might benefit from the findings, or even to NPA staff members who were not specialists in these fields.

Based on my professional experience over a 40-year period as a scientist and my participation in both basic and applied research, I believe that leaders in CONANP and administrators of NPAs should be strongly encouraged to support and enhance ongoing basic scientific research programs in NPAs. In reality, there often are some very direct economic benefits stemming from basic scientific research. In addition, ongoing scientific research can provide a sound foundation for successfully addressing many of the serious environmental problems currently facing us in Mexico and throughout the world. More broadly, a policy endorsing and encouraging basic scientific research in NPAs makes very good sense philosophically in terms of the long-term health and well-being of the biotic communities located there as well as for the people of Mexico.

Increasingly, the economic benefits of Mexico's NPAs to conservation economies of local communities and to the country as a whole are being recognized. In Mexico, NPAs cover about 24.5 million hectares—about 10% of its land area—and include about 1.3 million people living and working inside the NPAs (Bezaury-Creel and Pabon-Zamora, 2010). Considering solely their carbon storage, water supplies, and tourism activities, these protected areas are estimated to be worth about $3.4 billion per year. For every dollar invested in biodiversity conservation, at least $52 worth of benefits are generated for the economy; if all biodiversity values were included, the figure would be much higher (Bezaury-Creel and Pabon-Zamora, 2010). Ongoing basic scientific research could enhance these benefits. Some reviewers noted excessive government spending for local projects of questionable long-term value, arguing that such funds could be more effectively directed to basic scientific research.

However, besides economic benefits, I believe that basic scientific research is essential if we want to caringly and effectively confront climate change and other serious environmental problems, which are crises currently affecting the natural world. For too long, these problems have been minimized or ignored in all societies of the world. Yet just as in our efforts to cope with the challenging process of raising children, I believe that focusing solely on crisis management is not effective as a long-term strategy. The process of conscientiously and patiently endeavoring to understand and to caringly address the significant needs and issues affecting our children is essential to their long-term well-being. Similarly, I believe that basic scientific research should be a vital part of our long-term investment in the well-being of the natural environment and of all who depend on it.

Arguments for long-term strategies are well established. One well-known, long-term perspective toward the natural environment and its inhabitants is expressed eloquently by some indigenous Native American groups (http://www.sapphyr.net/natam/natam7philosophies.htm) who advocate, "Just as I would protect my own mother, so I will protect the Earth. I will ensure that the land, water, and air will be intact for my children and for my children's children—the unborn."

There are countless other examples that advocate taking a long-term perspective, including one in the UNESCO Earth Charter, which emphasizes an understanding (Principle 2) and a long-term improvement and maintenance (Principle 4) of the community of life (http://www.earthcharterinaction.org/content/pages/Read-the-Charter.htm). As these insights are better understood, they can be thoughtfully and effectively applied to achieve the difficult, yet important, balance between human needs and environmental well-being. Increasingly, results of past basic scientific research are being used effectively to address practical problems in the environment and in society (Velázquez et al., 2003, 2009).

I believe that knowledge resulting from basic scientific research provides an essential foundation for understanding and establishing a long-term, caring relationship with the environment and its inhabitants. As noted earlier, you cannot protect what you do not know. While basic scientific research often is a slow process and rarely provides quick answers, it ultimately provides the insights needed for living successfully and harmoniously within the natural environment over the long term. Those insights, of course, must be interpreted through caring ethical value systems.

Related to this proposal is the question of how ongoing basic scientific research programs might be established and encouraged in NPAs of Mexico. While many university researchers have been welcomed to conduct research in the NPAs, they often have their own specific research agendas and these may not be aligned very well with the needs of the NPA. Perhaps the administrators, Advisory Councils (Consejos Tecnicos Consultivos), and ecologists working within the NPAs best would be able to identify essential needs of NPAs over the long term. In many cases, NPA administrators have approached researchers at specific universities to request help with some of their priorities. However, rather than contacting only one or a few universities, communicating NPA priorities more broadly to the research communities of Mexico through, for example, a common website or other effective means of dissemination could stimulate interest in essential research topics to more than just one specific university.

A more complex matter that was pointed out by some reviewers is the egoism, pride, or personal interests and values that may be influencing key relationships and decisions. Even among researchers with overlapping interests or study sites, one reviewer noted that there often is a reluctance to share ideas with colleagues for fear that colleagues will use those ideas to gain a greater competitive edge for limited funding or may present those ideas as their own to gain professional stature. Differences in educational levels, practical experiences, personal familiarity with a region, use of professional intimidation, or personal and political friendships can complicate interpersonal communications considerably among CONANP leaders, NPA staff, university researchers and local people.

While such matters often cannot be resolved quickly or completely, these issues are very real and can be quite influential. Awareness and frank discussions about such topics, along with efforts to foster closer collaboration and mutual appreciation for the unique contributions each person can make, are essential components in dealing with these complex matters. One reviewer noted that greater involvement with the Advisory Councils in each NPA and more collaboration between these councils and the scientists or NGOs could alleviate some of the difficulties.

Another complex issue pointed out by one reviewer is the matter of safety for university researchers and NPA staff in some regions. In some NPAs, there is an ongoing low-level, illegal use of timber and other land resources by the local population. It can be awkward and even dangerous for researchers or NPA staff if they encounter groups involved in illegal activities while they are working on their projects.

In many cases, CONANP funding for research projects in NPAs is limited. This shortage of funds may be eased by having some NPA staff support made available in particular cases to assist in specific research projects, recognizing that some NPAs also are understaffed. Yet, clarifying the potential availability of staff support might encourage more interest in specific research projects.

However, another reviewer pointed out that this apparent shortage of funds in CONANP may not be as constraining as it seems since CONANP develops formal agreements with several agencies, including the National Commission for the Study and Conservation of Biodiversity (Comisión Nacional Para el Conocimiento y Uso de la Biodiversidad—CONABIO); the Ministry of Agriculture, Livestock, Rural Development, Fisheries, and Food (Secretaría de Agricultura, Ganadería, Desarrollo Rural, Pesca y Alimentación—SAGARPA); and the National Plant Genetic Resources for Food and Agriculture (Sistema Nacional de Recursos Fitogenéticos para la Alimentación y la Agricultura—SINAREFI). It also has informal agreements with the National Council for Science and Technology (Consejo Nacional de Ciencia y Tecnología—CONACYT). Thus, these agencies provide resources that also could be tapped to provide greater support for basic scientific research. One reviewer questioned the extent to which CONACYT considers NPAs as a funding priority for basic scientific research whereas another noted that they often want to help but must balance a variety of pressures and demands.

Certainly, closer communication and better collaboration between university researchers, NPA staff, and the local population are essential. Yet such communication and collaboration must be based on a clear expression of mutual appreciation for the assistance and support each sector gives to the other. It also is important that research results are available as soon as possible after the project has been completed with summaries also presented in a format and style readily understandable by the local communities and by the NPA professional staff. One reviewer suggested that CONANP should assume the primary responsibility for coordinating all of the basic scientific research activities in both federal and state protected areas through the formation of a new department.

In those cases where past experiences have diminished NPA administrators' desire to invite basic scientific researchers to conduct studies in an NPA, it could be helpful to establish formal agreements on previously contentious topics. Such agreements could describe the specific goals, methods, personnel to be used, and timing of a project, and they could clearly delineate the acceptable limits of the environmental impacts anticipated from the research. Agreements also could be negotiated concerning the projected deadline for making the research results available for use by the NPA. If some negotiated agreements were to result in the sharing of unpublished or unanalyzed data with an NPA administrator, there probably would need to be some strategy for maintaining confidentiality prior to the subsequent analysis of the data and publication of the final results. However, it seems to me, past issues could be addressed successfully among the involved professionals, and their efforts in addressing the issues openly would lead to the kind of working relationships needed to promote the benefits of scientific research as well as the effective management and overall health and well-being of the NPAs.

In summary, I propose that the CONANP leadership, in conjunction with the NPA Directors and their Advisory Councils, develop and implement management plans for every natural protected area in Mexico. Each plan should include descriptions of their key areas of interest, including the kinds of basic scientific research projects they consider important, in order of priority. CONANP could use its website to make these NPA plans and priorities for research available, and these could attract the attention of outside researchers in a manner that would promote a healthy competition for the implementation of each project.

As part of such programs, I believe that local communities should be clearly informed about outside research programs or other NPA activities that could affect them in any way, including the times and locations they can expect such activities to be occurring. Local communities also should receive clear and understandable explanations, in a timely fashion, about the significance of the results related to work conducted by NPA or by outside researchers.

University researchers can contribute to this process by taking more responsibility for providing results and for explaining the practical implications of their findings to NPA administrators and to the local communities in a timely and comprehensible manner. I also encourage both NPA staff and outside researchers to communicate clearly, patiently, and respectfully with local community members; it is very important to listen carefully and to respond honestly to each person's concerns. All parties involved with NPAs can contribute to a more effective collaborative process by openly and publicly acknowledging the contributions others have made to the success of their work.

I personally have been inspired by the high level of commitment and passion of the administrators and staff of protected lands here in Mexico and by their care and concern for the health and well-being both of the natural environments and of the communities of people living within them. It is readily apparent to me that Mexico is taking a leadership role in this effort. Equally, I am inspired by the passion and commitment of university researchers in Mexico who likewise are seeking the well-being of the land and its people. And, I also am inspired by the resiliency of the local communities and by their love for, and strong sense of connection with, their land. I sincerely believe that the sense of patrimony shared by all in Mexico would be enhanced considerably by stronger support for long-term basic scientific research programs in its NPAs. Such research programs would lay a more secure foundation for the management and long-term health of Mexico's unique and valuable natural protected areas.

Thus, I invite, welcome, and encourage continued discussion of this important topic among the leadership of CONANP; NPA administrators, staff, and Advisory Councils; NGOs; university researchers; community leaders and members; and all who are concerned about the long-term well-being and enduring national heritage of Mexico's Natural Protected Areas. I hope these ideas contribute positively to a serious dialogue that ultimately will result in the implementation of basic scientific research in NPAs—research that is based on new policies and on clear commitments by all those involved.

*Acknowledgments*: I greatly appreciate the insights that were shared with me in the numerous thoughtful comments I received from diverse reviewers, including Peace Corps Mexico (PCM) staff and volunteers, university researchers, and NPA staff and colleagues here in Mexico in response to an earlier draft of this article. Reviewers included: Ángel Piñeda (PCM Program Manager for Environment), PCM volunteers Chris Dudding (Sierra de Quila and Parque Nacional Volcán Nevado de Colima), Ryan Jensen (Sierra Gorda Biosphere Reserve, Guanajuato), Debbie Reid, Stacey Weller, and Sally Botzler (PCM Volunteer, Sierra Gorda Biosphere Reserve, Querétaro), as well as University researchers Marcela Araiza (Universidad Nacional Autónoma Mexico—UNAM), Liliana Cortes-Ortiz (University of Michigan, USA), Patricia Dávila (UNAM), Abril Gómez Barajas (UNAM), Edwin Gutiérrez (Universidad Autónoma de Yucatán), Gabriela Parra Olea (UNAM), Léia Scheinvar (UNAM), Alejandro Velázquez, (UNAM), Fernando Villaseñor (Universidad Michoacana de San Nicolás de Hidalgo) and two anonymous reviewers. Each person provided valuable commentary; however, I take full responsibility for any errors or misrepresentations of their ideas. I welcome all responses to *La Piñata* or directly to me at botzlerr@sbcglobal.net.

## Citations

Bezaury-Creel, Juan and Luis Pabon-Zamora, Editors. 2010. Valuing nature: Protected areas provide to the Mexican economy the equivalent of at least 52 dollars each dollar invested from the federal budget. *The Nature Conservancy*, 4 pp., http://www.nature.org/wherewework/ northamerica/mexico/files/valuing_nature_english.pdf.

Velázquez, Alejandro, Gerardo Bocco, Francisco J. Romero, and Azucena Pérez Vega. 2003. A Landscape Perspective on Biodiversity Conservation: The Case of Central Mexico. *Mountain Research and Development* 23(3): 240–246.

Velázquez, Alejandro, Eva M. Cué-Bär, Alejandra Larrazál, Neyra Sosa, José Luis Villaseñor, Michael McCall, Guillermo Ibarra-Manríquez. 2009. Building participatory landscape-based conservation alternatives: A case study of Michoacán, Mexico. *Applied Geography* 30: 1–14.

Author: Richard Botzler, Volunteer, Peace Corps Mexico, 2009–2011; Professor Emeritus, Department of Wildlife, Humboldt State University, Arcata, California 95519-8299, USA.

*(Note: Following our return to California, this article was sent to CONANP, which is the National Commission of Natural Protected Areas in Mexico. Although the US Postal Service verified its receipt by the CONANP office as well as the date it was received, there never was an official acknowledgment from CONANP or a response to the article.)*

# *Update 31*

## March 4, 2011

Hola, familia y amigos:

It was two years ago today that we flew from Washington, DC, to Mexico to begin our twenty-seven months of Peace Corps service. Now we are beginning our last three months—it just doesn't seem possible!

This past week we completed our official close-of-service (COS) activities, which included medical exams, health clearances, and well-organized meetings in Querétaro with the Peace Corps Mexico (PCM) staff. During the sessions we were guided in reflecting on our experiences as volunteers, in planning our final three months of activities, and in looking ahead to our return home as returned Peace Corps volunteers (RPCVs). Since COS was probably the last time our whole group of volunteers will be together, it was a particularly meaningful gathering for us.

We both have been very impressed with the high quality of support we have received as PCM volunteers. Our health care services have been excellent, and our safety and well-being have been given priority by the PCM staff. Likewise, our program leader, Ángel Piñeda, and his technical assistants, Benita Luna and Beatriz Charles, have provided strong support in preparing us to function effectively as volunteers and to make the most of this rich cultural and language-immersion experience. We hope many staff and fellow volunteers will visit us one day in California.

Attached are a few photos taken during our COS activities on Wednesday and Thursday, which coincided with the international kickoff of the fiftieth anniversary of Peace Corps. On Wednesday evening, former Peace Corps Mexico country director Byron Battle and his lovely wife Margarita hosted an anniversary party that was attended by several returned PCVs who live in the area as well as our group and the PCM staff. It was a festive and memorable evening!

Our plan is to return home to California the week of May 23. Following our return, we want to visit the three classes at Morris School that have been participating in the pen-pal program these past couple of years. We also have been invited to give presentations about our Peace Corps Mexico service to a few community organizations, and we look forward to those opportunities.

We are still waiting to hear whether CSU chancellor Charles Reed has approved international study programs in Mexico for 2011—including our three-week course in July on the Sierra Gorda and its distinctive approach to sustainable development with a conservation economy. We should be informed later this month. Hopefully, we will return to Mexico to introduce students to the important work that is continuing to progress in this green jewel in the heart of Mexico.

Truly, our own hearts are filled with gratitude and joy for all we have learned and for the new friends and experiences that have enriched our lives here in Mexico.

Con cariño,
Rick and Sally

# Update 32

## April 16, 2011

¡Hola, familia y amigos!

With only five weeks left in our Peace Corps Mexico (PCM) volunteer service, we are spending as much time as possible with Sierra Gorda and PCM colleagues and friends. We will miss them dearly and are encouraging folks to come visit us in California; we truly hope they will take us up on the invitation one day.

Close of service as Peace Corps volunteers involves us in writing final reports summarizing our work as well as filing the paperwork that will allow us to close our bank account, conclude our residency, and leave the country. As you can imagine, the process is a bit complicated and quite time-consuming!

Rick also is busy packing and mailing boxes of books and other items we want to keep that would put us over the weight limit in our luggage. It's amazing how much stuff we accumulated in twenty-seven months in Mexico, including cultural treasures with which we simply cannot part! Nonetheless, we are giving away a lot of things to women in the San Vicente community where Rick has been working. He is telling the women that the items are either for their own family use or for selling at fundraisers.

The crises in Japan following the massive earthquake and tsunami have captured the hearts of everyone in the world. We were grateful to hear that our friends and their families in Japan were not harmed, and we continue to hope and pray that the devastating problems still being experienced in the country will soon be resolved.

As we mentioned previously, the director of the Ecotourism Certificate Program at Humboldt State University, Michael Sweeney, and his wife Leslie came for a visit to the Sierra Gorda at the end of March. As a student in Michael's online courses, Sally has been focusing all her class assignments on the Sierra Gorda and on the efforts here to create community-based ecotourism as part of the commitment to an economy of conservation.

As he wrote in a recent announcement to other students in the course, Michael was impressed with Sally's descriptions of Sierra Gorda Ecotours, noting that he "saw it as a good template that could be replicated elsewhere to develop sustainable livelihoods for rural people." Ultimately, we had invited Michael, as he wrote, to "visit the area, experience some of the ecotour destinations first hand, and provide some observations and insights on the overall operation."

The tour with Michael and Leslie included a trip to Santa María de los Cocos and to the Sótano Del Barro (Mud Sinkhole). See photos at the following two links: http://sierragordaecotours.com/sitios-a-visitar/destinos-detalle.php?destino=25&lang=en and http://sierragordaecotours.com/sitios-a-visitar/destinos-detalle.php?destino=24.

Most of us rode mules for the two-hour, predawn ride up the steep mountainside, arriving for the sunrise and the stunning exhibition of squawking military macaws as they awakened from their night's sleep and flew in monogamous pairs up and out of the deep hole.

In addition to enjoying the natural environment during the trip, we made visits to four of the five Franciscan missions that are UNESCO World Heritage sites. All of us appreciated the fine work of Margarita Pedraza Muñoz in designing the itinerary and of Juan Manuel Garcia in guiding the tour. After returning home to California, Michael sent a thorough and detailed review of the complete tour. We're sure Michael's observations, evaluation, and recommendations will be very useful to Sierra Gorda Ecotours as staff work to make the region a world-class destination.

Immediately after Michael and Leslie left Jalpan, the two of us also took off for Querétaro to attend the third annual Peace Corps Mexico Biodiversity Forum. The forum provided exceptional learning opportunities about various strategies being used here in Mexico and throughout the world to address the effects of climate change, a relatively new area of Peace Corps emphasis in countries where volunteers are serving. We also had the opportunity to introduce thirty-one colleagues from the most recent group of PCM volunteers to the joys and challenges of teaching English as a second language. The hard work, enthusiastic participation, and thoughtful insights by the volunteers attending our session reflected their sense of the importance of this area of work and their commitment to it.

During the Biodiversity Forum, the two of us also selected a full-afternoon session on organic gardening, where we appreciated the chance for some hands-on practice with the double-digging approach. When we return to McKinleyville, we definitely will use the double-digging method in our organic garden! We hope to entice our young grandchildren to plant some of their favorite vegetables such as artichokes, which grow well along the coast.

We also are excited about presentations that we have set up with teachers at Morris School to share our PCM experience with the classes of children who have been participating in the pen-pal program these past two years. It will be a joy to deliver the children's last letters for the year along with their certificates of participation.

Next year, we will help the children continue connecting with their Sierra Gorda pen pals. In fact, our grandson Nate is going to be meeting his pen pal José Guadalupe face-to-face for the first time via Skype tomorrow!

Truly, our lives will never be the same after this rich cultural experience. Our Peace Corps Mexico service as volunteers has benefited us in more ways than we can ever know. We're grateful!

Con cariño,
Rick and Sally

# *Update 33*

## May 15, 2011

¡Hola, familia y amigos!

Today is Sunday, May 15—the Day of the Teacher here in Mexico. We warmly salute all teachers throughout the world with admiration, respect, and love.

The two of us feel a special gratitude for the teachers at the schools here in Jalpan de Serra—Benito Juárez, Melchor Ocampo, and Vicente Guerrero—and for the teachers at Morris School, the bilingual McKinleyville school where two of our grandchildren attend. All these teachers collaborated closely with us to support the correspondence between their students. It is very moving to think that this could be the beginning of lifetime international friendships between some of the pen pals.

We also are very grateful for the administrative support of the principals at each of these schools and for the assistance of our daughters Emi and Sarah, whose children are in participating classrooms. Without that support, we know the program couldn't have succeeded. ¡Muchas gracias!

As we've mentioned previously, our first project as returned Peace Corps volunteers will be to establish an Ecoclub in our community that is officially connected to the International Ecoclubs throughout the world. We also will be preparing for our return to Mexico in July 2012 to teach our class on the Sierra Gorda approach to sustainable development with a conservation economy. So we *want* to come back!

Sally and Rick in May 2011.

In reality, our hearts are brimming with appreciation for all we have learned during the two years of Peace Corps Mexico service. As is almost always the case, those involved in community service gain far more than they give. Have we mentioned that before?

Next week we will be back home in California. We will forever cherish memories of our special friends here in Mexico and do our best to maintain close connections with them. This is a poignant time for us.

Finally, our heartfelt thanks to each and every one of you on our list for the fabulous support you have extended to us during our PCM service. Your interest, encouragement, and many kindnesses have given us a deepened sense of connection with our family and friends in the United States, Germany, and Japan. ¡Muchas gracias!

Just as we are inviting our Mexican friends to come visit us in California, we also warmly invite each of you to come for a visit. We promise to share some of the treasures of the beautiful California Redwood Coast, as illustrated on this interactive online site made available by the National Park Service: https://www.nps.gov/redw/index.htm. Please come!

Con cariño,
Rick and Sally

# Update 34

## May 24, 2011
## Back Home in McKinleyville, California

¡Hola, familia y amigos!

This is just a final, quick note to let you know that we are safely home in McKinleyville, California. We now are returned Peace Corps volunteers (RPCVs). Again, our heartfelt thanks for the support you have extended to us during our twenty-seven months of Peace Corps Mexico service. We hope you will continue to keep in touch with us and maybe come visit us here in McKinleyville. As people in Mexico say, "¡Bienvenidos! ¡Nuestra casa es su casa!"

The weekend before our flight from the Benito Juárez International Airport in Mexico City, we visited the beautiful Basilica of Guadalupe on Saturday afternoon. The original basilica was built on the location of Juan Diego's vision of the Virgin of Guadalupe. See http://maryourmother. net/Guadalupe.html.

In 1979, Pope John Paul came for his celebrated first visit to Mexico, and he was welcomed lovingly by a children's choir that sang his favorite song, "Amigo," by Roberto Carlos. The YouTube video at the basilica is quite moving: http://www.youtube.com/watch?v=EVsaPC1MnuA&feature=related.

On Sunday afternoon, we got together with some of our Sierra Gorda friends in Mexico City and enjoyed a visit to the famous Frida Kahlo Museum followed by a traditional Mexican dinner and then an excursion to the canals at Xochimilco known for their colorful Venetian-style gondolas. Attached are a few weekend photos.

It was impossible for us to say "¡Adios!" to our many Sierra Gorda and Peace Corps Mexico friends. Instead, we said, "¡Nos vemos pronto!" ("See you soon!") and "¡Estaremos en contacto!" ("We will be in contact!")

Indeed, we hope to see many of you very soon. ¡Nos vemos pronto!

Con cariño,
Rick and Sally

# *Postscript*

Often, Rick and I have been asked, "What challenges did you encounter during your two years of Peace Corps service?" Like most Peace Corps volunteers, we certainly encountered challenges—some of which were rather difficult. But we seldom disclosed detailed descriptions of the hidden benefits and challenges we faced during our Peace Corps Mexico experience. Here they are!

### Assistance and Support of Family and School Colleagues

One important source of support during our two years of Peace Corps service in Mexico was that our eldest daughter, Emi, and her two young children, Olivia and Nelson, lived at our home in McKinleyville the entire time. Emi was employed, and she agreed to make the relatively small monthly mortgage payments for the house, in lieu of rent. Emi also paid for all the utilities during our absence. Whenever routine maintenance was needed, our contractor, Andy Lane, was readily available to assist.

Our youngest daughter, Sarah, and her son, Nate, also lived in McKinleyville during the two years of our Peace Corps service. Sarah purchased our 2007 Toyota Prius from us just prior to our departure. She was glad to have a smaller and more economical vehicle for her work as an itinerant home-health nurse, and we felt fortunate to have a buyer for our older vehicle.

Our grandchildren Olivia and Nate both attended Morris School, which had a Spanish-language immersion program at the time. Olivia and Nate were in the second and first grades, respectively, when we departed for our Peace Corps experience. Their teachers agreed to participate in the Spanish-language pen-pal program we organized between their classes at Morris and classes at a nearby school in the community where we served as PCVs.

Morris School principal Michael Davies-Hughes generously offered the necessary administrative support for the pen-pal program. Our two daughters, Emi and Sarah, provided the essential links with the children's classes and teachers, duplicating and distributing the templates for the pen-pal correspondence and collecting and mailing the completed letters to us in Mexico. We could not have sustained the pen-pal program without their regular assistance.

During the two years, we kept in touch with our five children and with many of our grandchildren, as well as with my sisters and a large number of friends, via e-mail and face-to-face Skype time. Skype is a free Internet service requiring only computer access. It was a joy to see our loved ones via Skype whenever it could be arranged!

In December 2009, we were able to fly home to McKinleyville for Christmas and the New Year. Then, in June 2010, we hosted as many of our children and grandchildren as possible for a family vacation in Guadalajara and Zacatecas, Mexico. Our son Thomas and his wife Lisa were able to come along with all four of their young-adult children and two of their friends. In addition, our daughter Emi came with Olivia and Nelson, and our daughter Sarah came with

Nate. Altogether, there were fifteen of us. Our son Tin came from Los Angeles to visit us in Jalpan for Christmastime 2010. All of these family visits were a source of joy for us!

## Unanticipated Financial Benefits

As is usual for all PCVs, the Peace Corps provided a regular stipend for our basic living expenses in Mexico. The stipend is intended to allow PCVs to pay for essential needs only.

Surprisingly (it truly took us by *complete* surprise), we discovered that our bank account in the United States was automatically accumulating our monthly pensions and social security payments. Thus, we were able to enhance our savings account considerably during our two years of Peace Corps service. We truly had not expected that we would be gaining so much financially as PCVs.

Consequently, we were able to pay by ourselves for the costs of most of our special Peace Corps projects—such as the pen-pal exchange program—without relying on additional Peace Corps funding. Although Rick applied for and received a small amount of funding for his amphibian research project, all of our other Peace Corps projects were self-funded. This gave us the flexibility to purchase a color printer, which we connected to the laptop computer we had brought with us from the United States. The printer was essential for our successful pen-pal program.

## Challenges of Learning Spanish

Although I had been studying Spanish since 2004—including intensive study in Oaxaca, Mexico, in summer 2006—Rick was new to Spanish. Both of us were native English speakers. However, Rick also was fluent in German, and German was my "first second" language. But even with good effort, Rick found it especially difficult to learn Spanish. In my case, I frequently confused German and Spanish phrases—and still do today.

Subsequently, when Rick and I visited friends and relatives in Germany, shortly after our two years in Mexico, I found it nearly impossible to communicate in German without inserting words and phrases in Spanish. Often, Rick took over and interpreted what I was trying to say.

In reality, my Peace Corps service included quite a lot of translation work. I translated documents from Spanish to English and from English to Spanish with increasing success. In my English-language classes for staff at our site, I developed friendships that will last a lifetime. I also learned what it means to speak "Spanglish" during conversations with Mexican friends. Whenever we friends were discussing complicated or sensitive personal topics, each of us would automatically revert to our primary languages or a mixture of Spanish and English—Spanglish!

## Coping with Intensive Preservice Preparation

Our preservice preparation program in the city of Querétaro, Mexico, was intensive—and sometimes quite stressful. Living at the time with our wonderful host family was greatly beneficial, and we have sustained a very close relationship with Lupe and Antonio ever since. Their whole family extended a generosity of spirit and kindhearted support that made all the difference for us.

The conversations in Spanish with our host family ranged widely—from personal issues, such as international adoption laws, to history, geography, economics, religion, and even politics. We felt fortunate to be benefiting from their knowledge and experience. Antonio coached us on good manners in Mexico too. One time when he asked me if I would like more of something, I replied, "Gracias, no." Antonio explained that I needed to say, "No, gracias," so there would be no confusion. Antonio's and Lupe's humor created a very positive learning environment for us.

Most of our preservice classes and workshops took place at the Peace Corps office in Querétaro. The Peace Corps administrators and staff members were strongly supportive in helping us become integrated within the Mexican cultural and language environment. The friendly yet firm guidance we PCVs received was quite amazing! The staff members were highly professional in helping all of us become ready to serve as Peace Corps volunteers in Mexico. Our Spanish-language abilities and our cultural understanding were strengthened daily.

## Dealing with Personalities of Other PCVs and PC Staff

Of course, we also experienced some conflicts with Peace Corps staff and our fellow volunteers. Personality differences posed challenges that were sometimes frustrating. Most of the time, most of us got along well. The occasional disagreements usually were handled with respect and courtesy. Ultimately, every one of our particular preservice group of volunteers was officially sworn in for Peace Corps service; however, a few people left after only a short time in their placement sites.

Throughout the two years, the Peace Corps Mexico staff offered several opportunities for us volunteers to strengthen our knowledge and skills. The regular workshops and conferences were of great help to us. We needed to fulfill our pledge of service and adhere to all the Peace Corps expectations and rules as part of this US government program. Perhaps not surprisingly, this included abiding by medical requirements for regular checkups and immunizations.

Just prior to our swearing-in ceremony, there was an international flu epidemic that apparently started in Mexico. It was very reassuring to witness the quick responses of the Mexican government and of the Peace Corps in protecting the health and well-being of the general population, including all of us PCVs. The US Peace Corps alert system and the supportive relationship with the offices in Washington, DC, were reassuring benefits of our experience as volunteers in Mexico. (All of us volunteers were given flu antidotes, just in case we became ill.)

## Adjusting to Our Service Community

We felt extremely fortunate to be placed in the beautiful Sierra Gorda Biosphere Reserve for our Peace Corps service. The primary organization to which we were assigned was Grupo Ecológico, or the Ecological Group. The director of the Ecological Group was Pati Ruíz Corzo, who had overseen the organization for over two decades at the time we arrived in the town of Jalpan de Serra in the northern part of the state of Querétaro.

Pati was, and still is, a model of committed service to environmental responsibility and sustainability. We gained immeasurably from our Peace Corps affiliation with Pati and her staff members. Pati's connection with worldwide environmentalists, such as Bill McKibben and Al Gore, reflected her capacity for building consensus and for fulfilling the goals of her organization. Pati and her team successfully funded projects in restoration and preservation with a conservation economy that is a remarkable model for worldwide replication. Pati and her staff already had secured donations and private foundation grants exceeding $45,000,000 at the time of our arrival.

Nonetheless, our adjustment to this service community included challenges. For example, Rick's background in wildlife biology was deemed somewhat irrelevant to the Ecological Group's vision and mission. Rick's efforts to encourage the incorporation of the scientific method and field research projects were met with strong resistance. This, along with Rick's limited Spanish skills, ultimately resulted in his being "reassigned" to projects different from those he'd originally expected. These changes were challenging for both of us!

## Setting Up Our Temporary Home

Soon after our arrival, Rick and I developed a comfortable domestic routine. Overall, our adjustment to life in Jalpan was quite pleasant. All of the Sierra Gorda staff members helped us considerably in our adjustment and in feeling connected to project activities. In particular, Margarita Pedraza Muñoz provided very strong support to us, for which we will be eternally grateful. She took us all over the region to experience the extraordinarily beautiful environment, to meet women entrepreneurs who were developing new eco-businesses, and to share insights with us about her own part in the Sierra Gorda–focused work. Her home community also was a remarkable demonstration of environmental responsibility and sustainability. Since Margarita had been an English major at Cambridge and had been married to a Brit, she was fluent in English, which helped us communicate with her about our perplexing questions and concerns.

I am embarrassed to confess that my response to some of the more intense stressors during our Peace Corps service in the Sierra Gorda involved my drinking more alcohol than ever before in my life. Whereas Rick enjoyed sampling Mexican beers, I found the white wines of Mexico quite appealing at the end of the workday. My drinking developed into a pattern that I came to regret.

One of the most beneficial aspects of our adjustment to the Jalpan community was the hiring of our wonderful housekeeper, Siria. Siria came every Saturday morning to clean the entire house. She dusted all the furniture and wet-mopped all the floors, which continuously accumulated layers of dust blown in from the streets and yards. While Siria cleaned, I did the laundry for the week in our old-fashioned washer that had two compartments: one for washing and rinsing and one for spinning out the residual water. I routinely filled buckets with the wash and rinse waters, which Siria reused on the slate floors and outdoor walkways. I then hung the laundry in our backyard to dry. On rainy days, Rick strung clotheslines in our covered, open-air kitchen.

Each and every Saturday, while Siria and I were hard at work in the house together, Rick did the grocery shopping. These forays out into the community greatly aided Rick's Spanish-language development. Also, he became acquainted with all the produce vendors and the shopkeepers in Jalpan. Rick became a very competent shopper!

Occasionally, the two of us attended mass at the Catholic mission church just down the street from us. It was a joy to see whole families together at church—from the tiniest newborns to the most elderly great-grandparents; the multigenerational congregational gatherings were remarkable to us—unlike US churches, which increasingly are becoming less well attended.

Rick and I also were enchanted by the liveliness of community gatherings at the central plaza, which regularly included Huapango music and dancing. Our exposure to the local schools allowed us to become recognizable temporary residents of the Jalpan community. Children who had seen us in their school classrooms often greeted us warmly when they encountered us on the streets. Occasionally, children asked us when the next set of pen-pal letters would be coming.

## Tropical-Climate Insects

Rick knew that I thoroughly disliked having tropical insects in our home. Yuck! He became increasingly skillful at whacking them and disinfecting surfaces where they had been crawling.

## Finding a Good Fit for Our Service in the Field

At the start we felt a bit uncertain about what our Peace Corps Mexico service would entail, and the Sierra Gorda Ecological Group administrators and staff probably also were a bit perplexed about what to do with us—what we could do effectively in support of their program vision and mission. We truly did our very best to be flexible, cooperative, and cheerful during the process of finding a good fit for our areas of service.

During our preservice preparation, Peace Corps Mexico staff member Regina Montaño had emphasized the importance of PCVs' flexibility (*flexibilidad*). We came to see that she was absolutely right about that! In addition, Regina explained that in Mexico it was more polite to refer to communicating with others not as "discussing with" (*discutir con*) but rather as "talking with" (*platicar con*). I appreciated this distinction, and it was helpful to me ever after.

## Getting Support for Our Pen-Pal Program

Starting an international pen-pal program between elementary students at schools in our town of Jalpan in the Sierra Gorda and students at the Spanish-immersion school in McKinleyville, where two of our grandchildren were young students, was an appealing idea to us.

I myself had some personal experience as a pen pal. When I was in seventh grade, my teacher was in contact with the principal at a Lutheran academy for girls in Germany. The girls in my class were given the opportunity to be matched with a pen pal. My German friend, Heidi Nieden, and I have been pen pals now for over sixty years.

When our pen-pal friendship began, Heidi was fifteen years old, and I was twelve. Heidi had learned enough English by then to write letters to me in English. Once I began studying German in high school, I did my best to write to Heidi in German. When the two of us were college students and our time was more limited, we reverted to writing in our primary languages, trusting that each of us would be able to comprehend well enough.

Heidi and I enjoyed our first face-to-face meeting in September 1981, when our family accompanied Rick for his Fulbright fellowship at the University of Hohenheim near Stuttgart—only a couple hours' drive to the Nurnberg suburb where Heidi's family was living at the time. It was a joy to me that our two families got along so well and that we were able to spend time together at one another's homes and at some of the beautiful cultural sites in southern Germany. During the 1981–1982 year, our families got together on thirteen different occasions!

Thus, when we learned about Peace Corps goals 2 and 3, Rick and I began thinking about the possibility of establishing a pen-pal program as one of our supplementary PCV projects. It occurred to us that supporting international friendships that begin in childhood can be very impactful. We thought carefully about our purpose as volunteers in Mexico.

Again, the Peace Corps' mission is "to promote world peace and friendship by fulfilling three goals":

1. To help the people of interested countries in meeting their need for trained men and women.
2. To help promote a better understanding of Americans on the part of the peoples served.
3. To help promote a better understanding of other peoples on the part of Americans.

Addressing goals 2 and 3 through a pen-pal program seemed highly relevant to us—as well as a potentially enjoyable supplementary project. As a professional educator, I was familiar with school settings and the basic requirements for starting an educational program in local schools.

Our Peace Corps' program manager, Ángel Piñeda, approved our proposed pen-pal program as a supplementary project, and the director of the Ecological Group to which we were assigned in Jalpan, Mexico, also supported our idea. Since Director Pati Ruíz Corzo had been a professional educator herself, she had established strong environmental education programs throughout the Sierra Gorda region. Our proposed pen-pal program seemed to be a good fit as a PCV project.

Establishing the pen-pal program was complicated. Two women who oversaw the Ecological Group's environmental education programs helped us enormously. Lulú and Olivia helped us make our initial contacts and appointments with the school principals, introduced us as Peace Corps volunteers, and paved the way for me to meet with the principals to seek their approval of the pen-pal program. Principals at two schools, which conveniently were just down the street from where we lived in Jalpan, responded very enthusiastically about our proposed international pen-pal program. They each identified teachers who might be interested in the project.

The principal at Morris School in our hometown of McKinleyville also was supportive of the idea. Michael Davies-Hughes had been receiving our regular e-mail updates and was familiar with our Peace Corps service. Since Morris was a Spanish-immersion school, Michael agreed that our proposed international pen-pal program could be a positive experience for the classes in which our two grandchildren were enrolled. He spoke with the teachers, and they agreed to participate. Based on a recommendation from another PCV, Rick took on the Birds Beyond Borders pen-pal project, and Michael connected Rick with a fourth-grade teacher at Morris.

Thus, Rick and I had three classrooms of children at Morris to match with three classrooms at the local Jalpan schools. The teachers had classes in grades one, two, and four. Rick worked with the two fourth-grade teachers in starting his part of the project, and I worked with the first- and second-grade teachers. During the nearly two years of our project, Rick and I developed warm relationships with the teachers and their school administrators. All were very supportive, cooperative, and enthusiastic about the pen-pal program.

To facilitate the correspondence, I routinely developed templates in Spanish that children in all the classes could use for their letters. At the beginning, the templates focused on getting-to-know-you communications. The Morris classes had school pictures that we were able to glue onto the letters, and Rick and I took individual and group photos of the Jalpan classes to share with the Morris pen pals. Naturally, we followed all school regulations about sharing photos and personal information in the pen-pal exchanges. The principals and teachers assured compliance.

First and foremost, we did our best to make sure that every child in every class was matched with a pen pal and that each student sent and received a letter every time. In order to keep accurate records that documented full participation of the students in all classes, we routinely made copies on the color printer we had purchased for this purpose, and we kept copies of all letters in class portfolios inside sturdy binders. At the end of each year, we distributed decorative certificates of participation as well as gifts of bilingual books for each teacher in each class.

Our daughters Emi and Sarah helped us enormously by arranging with the first- and second-grade teachers at Morris to drop off packets of letters from us in Jalpan and then to pick up the Morris children's letters and mail them to us. Rick and I handled these tasks with the teachers at the Jalpan schools. Not unexpectedly, it was sometimes necessary to return to the classrooms to pick up letters from children who might have been absent for some reason on the day the class was doing the letter writing. The teachers were amazingly patient and helpful in making sure each child wrote and received a letter.

We discovered that mail service between the United States and Mexico was quite poor. For a while, we switched from the postal service to FedEx. One of the administrators at the Sierra Gorda Ecological Group used a courier to send and receive important communications and equipment. He generously allowed us to send and receive our packets of letters.

With the help of another employee in the Ecological Group, we were able to sustain the pen-pal program after our two years in the Sierra Gorda. However, the courier service was no longer available at that time, and we agreed to stop the pen-pal program. I felt disappointed about that!

**Frustrations and Stressors**

In addition to the challenges of maintaining the pen-pal program, Rick and I were deeply involved in our primary assignments as PCVs in the Sierra Gorda. My responsibilities involved translation work, and this was time-consuming but quite satisfying. I worked very hard every day.

Rick also worked very hard on his assigned projects. However, Rick's responsibilities as a PCV did not give him any chance to apply his professional knowledge and skills in the biological sciences, in wildlife management, or in environmental ethics. The director and administrators in the Ecological Group wanted volunteers, including Rick and me, to assist in already-established projects that were the primary focus of the group's efforts to create a conservation economy through restoration and preservation activities.

In essence, Rick's interest in basic scientific research was thwarted. The negativity about scientific research was disappointing to him. Nonetheless, Rick was able to connect with fellow scientists in Mexico, and he successfully collaborated with them and, in fact, gave professional presentations in Spanish in other places in Mexico. However, none of this work seemed to be viewed positively by the Ecological Group director and administrators, and that was stressful.

One of Rick's assignments was to support the efforts of the Ecoclub coordinator. When helping with plans for an on-site Ecoclub leadership workshop that would be assembling approximately one hundred youth from throughout the Sierra Gorda, Rick asked to present information to them about the chytrid fungus in amphibians. The coordinator heartily agreed, and Rick was excited about the opportunity. He did his best to create a stimulating slide talk in Spanish for the Ecoclub youth. However, on the morning of Rick's presentation, the coordinator left the room to attend to other responsibilities. The Ecoclub youth were attentive and fascinated by the presentation, but Rick realized there would be no chance for any follow-up projects, given the coordinator's lack of interest.

It was very satisfying for Rick to make connections with other scientists in Mexico, including professors who were actively conducting research on wildlife diseases such as the chytrid fungus. However, it also was frustrating and stressful for him to have his professional knowledge and skills dismissed and even maligned by the Sierra Gorda Ecological Group's director and administrators.

## Bouts of Temporary Illness

Other than occasional bouts of diarrhea, Rick stayed well throughout our twenty-seven months in Mexico. However, I experienced a few different illnesses and health problems, all of which were addressed by the Peace Corps medical officer. The several, yet short-lived, health issues I experienced were diarrhea (including an explosive variety one time), UTIs, the flu, a leg injury that was treated by a marvelous orthopedic physician, and the onset of wide-angle glaucoma, which was treated by a marvelous ophthalmologist. Regular physical and dental checkups as well as required immunizations were all a routine part of our Peace Corps experience in Mexico. We were grateful!

## Conflicts with Counterparts

Not surprisingly, we occasionally experienced conflicts with our Peace Corps counterparts. As described in more detail previously, Rick was unable to convince the director and the administrators at the Sierra Gorda Ecological Group of the potential benefits of engaging in independent scientific research.

Rick's proposed scientific study of amphibians throughout the Sierra Gorda to determine the presence and prevalence of the devastating worldwide incidence of the chytrid fungus was flat-out rejected. Rick's idea about involving youth who were involved in the Sierra Gorda Ecoclubs also was opposed. One key administrator, although an outstanding nature photographer and good naturalist, was adamant that fieldwork with youth would be very dangerous. Rick felt quite limited and ultimately realized the need to forgive our counterparts and work independently with other professionals.

Fortunately, the Peace Corps Mexico directors and program leaders were empathetic and supportive throughout our entire twenty-seven-month placement in the Sierra Gorda. In fact, some of them told us how they too had sometimes been treated rudely and even contemptuously by these particular counterparts. It seemed quite unfortunate to Rick and me that these conflicts ultimately led to the withdrawal of the Sierra Gorda Ecological Group from further participation with the Peace Corps Mexico program.

## Getting Fired—*Despedida*

In Spanish, the word *despedida* has two different connotations: a retiring or firing! When Rick was terminated from the Sierra Gorda Ecological Group by the director, it was a somewhat traumatic *despedida* for both of us. Our Peace Corps program manager, Ángel Piñeda, was supportive and kind as he supported and assisted Rick with the necessary changes.

Rick's new areas of service included working one Saturday morning per month with a group of community youth and helping prepare them to be ecotourism guides for English-speaking tourists. Rick also worked once a week with university students and faculty in a college-level ecotourism preparation program, which included development of English-language skills. Also, Rick assisted an elementary school teacher/principal with science and English lessons every Wednesday. Given Rick's trepidation about his adequacy for this role and his lack of prior experience working with young children, we came to call these days "Wild Wednesdays."

### Being Labeled "Loose Cannons"

During a routine site visit, shortly after Rick's *despedida*, the new PCM country director's wife initiated a philosophical conversation with Rick about what a prisoner might do after being unfairly imprisoned. The PCM country director casually wandered over to listen to Rick's response. After about ten minutes of an interesting and spirited discussion, Rick sensed that he was being checked out to assess his possible anger over the *despedida*. Although Rick didn't alter any of his responses, he wondered whether the director might consider him a loose cannon within the Peace Corps community since Rick had previously overheard the director using this label for PCVs who were "difficult." (Rick hoped that he had passed this test!)

### Missing Our Family

Rick and I deeply love our children and grandchildren. Being away from them for twenty-seven months of Peace Corps Mexico service was difficult for us. We did our best to maintain contact with family and friends through regular e-mail and Skype contact, but it just wasn't the same as personal interaction. At the end of a Skype connection, I often said, "I wish I could hug you!" Those times during our period of Peace Corps service when we could be together with family and friends were very important to us.

### Hosting a Family Vacation in Mexico

We had a particularly enjoyable family experience in June 2010 when we hosted our children and grandchildren for a vacation in Guadalajara and Zacatecas. Rick and I booked rooms at a hotel with a swimming pool in Guadalajara, and it was great fun to swim and goof around with the family in the pool. A carriage ride provided our group with a tour of central Guadalajara, which has beautiful historical buildings and statues.

We also enjoyed seeing the sights at Mexico's largest natural lake just south of Guadalajara. At the shore of Lake Chapala, we shared a delicious Father's Day dinner while being serenaded by a dynamic Mexican mariachi band. After dinner, we took boat rides to an island in the lake. It was a lovely experience.

Rick and I had rented two large vans that comfortably accommodated our group of fifteen. The sights along the drive to Zacatecas were enchanting. In Zacatecas, we enjoyed riding a small train while visiting a silver mining operation. Rick and I distributed souvenir money to each family member so that everyone could choose something special in the street markets.

Our family also toured the central plaza with its huge statue of Pancho Villa as well as a well-known chapel that is dedicated to the value of work. People frequently come to this chapel to give their prayers of thanks for their work and to offer petitions for work they need.

## Extending and Enjoying Hospitality in Our Community

During our two years in Jalpan, we frequently hosted guests in our home and at the Sierra Gorda grounds. For example, we hosted a baby shower (*lluvia de regalos*) via Skype for Buffy and Ben Lenth, the couple who had worked as PCVs in the Sierra Gorda and had lived in our house before returning to Colorado with their beautiful dog Chavo. The baby shower was well attended, and the Skype connection was excellent during the event. The games, prepared and led by one of the Lenth's best friends at the Sierra Gorda offices, were hilarious. The many gifts the couple's friends brought were packaged and mailed via the special courier service. It was fun!

Rick and I also hosted an evening of Huapango music and dancing that was entertaining for all of us. We had a celebration of the Chinese New Year and put a chart of the twelve Chinese animals for the year at our doorway for guests to sign as they arrived. Then we served favorite Chinese dinners, delivered by a young man on a motorcycle from the local Chinese restaurant. In Jalpan, this particular Chinese restaurant was a favorite!

In addition to monthly gatherings in our home, we also co-hosted a festive Thanksgiving dinner for our friends at the Sierra Gorda grounds. The Peace Corps Mexico country director and his wife, Dan and Julia Evans, brought the turkey, which was roasted in our home oven.

Rick and I also enjoyed the wonderful occasions for which we were invited to the homes of Sierra Gorda friends. We attended a traditional Day of the Dead dinner as well as a traditional Posada Christmas dinner. Both were very special occasions with a lot of conversation and joy.

One friend in particular, Margarita Pedraza Muñoz, often hosted us at her lovely home in one of the more remote communities just outside Jalpan. Margarita has created an ecologically responsible and sustainable home environment on her property, including ecotourist lodging, a huge organic garden, an effective composting system, dry toilets, a solar water heater, and much more—along with a beautiful small cottage made of local stones that she built and now occupies.

On one return trip to Mexico as RPCVs, we stayed at Margarita's comfortable ecotourist house, and she helped us arrange to host a dinner for many of our local Sierra Gorda friends and their families, with the services of a local caterer. It was a happy reunion!

## Hosting New Ecotourism Colleagues

While still in Jalpan, toward the end of our twenty-seven-month period of service, Rick and I had the pleasure of hosting the professor for my Ecotourism Certificate Program from Humboldt State University. Michael Sweeney and his wife Leslie stayed with us about a week, so that we could accompany them in experiencing the guided tour of various sites in the Sierra Gorda that I had included as part of the required project for Michael's final course. The tour is titled "Educational Ecotourism Experience: Sustainable Development in the Sierra Gorda." Michael and Leslie became friends of ours through this enjoyable experience.

## And the Beat Goes On …

Upon our return to our home community in McKinleyville, California, it was a joy to reconnect with our children, grandchildren, and friends. Also, Rick and I endeavored to build on our rich Peace Corps Mexico experiences. Although the following descriptions are rather brief, we continue to be involved in addressing Peace Corps goals 2 and 3 within our home community.

## Sharing Our Peace Corps Experiences

Rick and I frequently were invited to share our experiences as PCVs in Mexico with gatherings of interested groups throughout our home community. A group of seniors participating in the Osher Lifelong Learning Institute at Humboldt State University was among the first to invite us to present. Several seniors had been PCVs as young adults, and the discussion was enriched by their shared experiences.

## Continuing Our Pen-Pal Program

In fall 2011, immediately following our return to our home community of McKinleyville, Rick and I began serving as grandparent volunteers at the Morris immersion school in the classes of our three grandchildren, Olivia (third grade), Nate (second grade), and Nelson (kindergarten). Rick also volunteered in the class that had participated as fourth graders in his Birds Beyond Borders pen-pal program—now a sixth-grade class.

Before we left Mexico, Rick and I had identified a Sierra Gorda friend who graciously agreed to help us continue the international pen-pal program in which her daughter had been participating at one of the schools in Jalpan. I continued to develop the Spanish-language templates for the letters, and we facilitated the letter-writing process at Morris and provided the funds needed for our friend in the Sierra Gorda to distribute the letters from Morris students and collect and mail the letters from students at the schools in Jalpan.

We soon realized that our friend simply didn't have time to return to the classrooms there in Jalpan to ensure that each child had completed a letter before sending the class packets of letters to us. Thus, not every student in our participating classes of pen pals at Morris routinely received a letter. Initially, I was able to deal with this problem by duplicating some of the letters and adding the names of those students whose original pen pals had not been able to complete a letter for them.

This problem was exacerbated by even more serious issues with the mail service between Mexico and the United States. Ultimately, we could not overcome these issues, and at the end of the 2011–2012 school year, the pen-pal program needed to be ended. We were quite disappointed about that.

## Starting the Bilingual McKinleyville Ecoclub

With the support and assistance of Morris School's principal, Michael Davies-Hughes, and the Morris teachers, Rick and I made plans to launch one of the first Ecoclubs in the United States— the Bilingual McKinleyville Ecoclub. Michael asked us to attend a school district board of trustees meeting, and he placed an item on that month's agenda concerning the proposed Ecoclub. Rick and I were very pleased that the board approved our starting the club. This approval allowed the new Ecoclub to have access to classroom space for on-campus afternoon meetings along with the liability insurance required for students to be able to participate.

That fall, we formed a group of Morris parents to assist with the development of the Ecoclub. The initial group of more than ten parents met with us at our home in October 2011. We had been told by the Ecoclub coordinator in the Sierra Gorda that there were US Ecoclubs getting started in El Paso, Texas. I contacted the national US Ecoclub coordinator, Sylvia Sillas, and she invited me to come to El Paso and connect with Ecoclub facilitators there. I traveled to El Paso in March 2012, shortly after Rick and I had begun holding Ecoclub meetings at Morris School.

Michael ultimately became the McKinleyville Union School District superintendent, and he continued his strong support of our efforts to establish an Ecoclub at Morris. He suggested that Rick and I become part-time district employees so that we could supervise after-school and off-campus Ecoclub activities without the assistance of other school district staff members. Thus, after our background checks, Rick and I were given part-time assignments and paid for our two to three hours per week as greeters when children arrived at school. We really enjoyed greeting the children and their parents at the start of the school day at Morris, and it gave us the chance to connect regularly with new Ecoclub members as well.

Currently, the Bilingual McKinleyville Ecoclub is certified by Ecoclubs International as an official Ecoclub. Our projects have increased and diversified over the past several years.

**Connecting with the National and International Ecoclub Organization**

Our Ecoclub development benefited greatly from the support of Dr. Gustavo Iturralde, a consultant with the Pan American Health Organization (PAHO) offices in El Paso. PAHO is the Latin American arm of the World Health Organization.

Ever since Ecoclubs began in Argentina in 1992, PAHO has strongly supported their development and expansion. Dr. Iturralde and US Ecoclubs promoter Sylvia Sillas, as well as Sylvia's assistant Edmundo Rodríguez, came to McKinleyville in 2012 and again in 2013, to provide in-person support and to help lead and participate in our first Ecoclub Youth Leadership Workshop. With our assistance, Gustavo developed the first and only bilingual guide for US Ecoclubs, which we now are adapting to reflect changing conditions in US Ecoclubs.

Unfortunately, the El Paso PAHO office was closed in 2014 due to perceptions of some administrators at the US Department of Health and Human Services that PAHO's services were redundant and unneeded. Our loss of Gustavo's support was significant. With Edmundo as the new national Ecoclub promoter for the United States, we are sustaining our Bilingual McKinleyville Ecoclub. Also, our Ecoclub Leadership Team has been working to expand the number of Ecoclubs in our local area and in the larger North Coast California community.

**Return Trips to Mexico**

Rick and I have returned to Mexico a few times since completing our Peace Corps service. On each occasion, it has been a joy to reconnect with the Peace Corps staff in the city of Querétaro, with our host family there, and with our friends and colleagues in the Sierra Gorda and in Mexico

City. We also enjoyed visiting historic sites in Mexico City that had been off-limits to us during our Peace Corps service due to safety and security concerns.

## Hosting Friends from Mexico in Our Home

I have sustained e-mail connections with many of our Mexican friends. In this way, I have continued to develop my Spanish-language skills and a strong commitment to the continuous improvement of my fluency.

It also has been a great joy for Rick and me to host Mexican friends here in our home in McKinleyville. Prior to our departure, we warmly welcomed several friends from Peace Corps Mexico and the Sierra Gorda to visit us.

In January 2012, our Mexican friend Óscar Estrada came to McKinleyville for a week-and-a-half-long visit. Óscar had been the accountant for the Sierra Gorda Ecological Group and also one of the star students in my advanced English-language class there. He is someone with whom I greatly enjoy Spanglish conversations that range broadly on diverse topics.

Despite the rainy January weather, Rick and I took Óscar to all our favorite places on the North Coast. We showed him the Humboldt State University campus and the buildings in which we had taught classes, the amazing redwood forests and trails, the rugged coastline and beaches, and the quaint Victorian village of Ferndale. We took him to some of our favorite restaurants.

During his first visit (also his very first flight), Rick and I enjoyed introducing Óscar to our family and to our Ecoclub friends. I also took Óscar to my Spanish-conversation class at HSU. The professor put him on the spot (the "hot seat") and engaged him in a question-and-answer session with the large group of students. Óscar was quite nervous about this experience, but he easily maintained his composure and good humor. Likewise, Óscar visited with several classes at Morris School, and the children had many interesting questions for him. This visit gave the children an authentic communication experience in Spanish, which Óscar obviously enjoyed.

Then, in January 2016, Óscar came to California once again and this time brought his wife, Dani, and their two adorable children, Rubí and David. We rented a van and took the whole family to most of the same places we had visited with Óscar on his first visit. The couple now has a third child, and Óscar sends us photos of his dear family. We stay in touch!

# Appendix A

**My Peace Corps Application Cross-Cultural Experience Statement (Essay 1)**

*Peace Corps Volunteers must be open to ideas and cultures different from their own and may need to modify their appearance or behavior appropriately. Give an example (between 250–500 words) of a significant experience that illustrates your ability to adapt in an unfamiliar environment. Please highlight the skills you used and the perspectives you gained. You may draw from experiences in your work, school, or community in the U.S. or abroad. Please list the date(s) of your experience.*

In late May through early July 2006, I participated in a five-week language and cultural immersion program in Oaxaca, Mexico. I lived with a wonderful host family while enrolled at the University in Oaxaca (UABJO). While there, I completed intensive Spanish III-level courses in conversation and composition as well as a course in Mexican history that included several field trips to archeological sites in the region.

My coursework also included service-learning projects with children in two of the outlying communities near Oaxaca: a program of English Second Language activities and an after-school sports program. Although I am not Catholic, each Sunday I enjoyed attending an evening mass with the mother and the maid servant of my host family.

The family also included me in social events and celebrations that allowed me to become better acquainted with everyone involved. I learned an enormous amount in these experiences. The extended personal interactions and my extracurricular experiences complemented, extended, and enriched what I gained from the formal program of study at the University.

Throughout the entire time that I was living and studying in Oaxaca, there was a strike and several massive protest marches by the state's teachers and other public employees who set up camps and literally lived in the streets for months, using only tarps for protection from the sun and rain. Thus, the streets in the center of the city were effectively blockaded, and only pedestrians could traverse them. Incidents of violence occasionally occurred. I kept well informed on the key issues by reading local and international newspapers on a daily basis.

Although some of the professors at the University stressed that we students should be cautious and should avoid walking through areas where the strikers were encamped, I was always able to comfortably and respectfully navigate the streets without the slightest fear for my own personal safety. On one occasion I had to ask to be permitted to pass a street blockade, and I said simply, but directly, "Yo quisiera pasar, por favor." And then I said, sincerely, "Gracias."

Not surprisingly, others in the community held diverse opinions about the teachers who were striking. As my understanding increased concerning the political and economic conditions that led to the strike, I empathized with the teachers' positions.

At the same time, members of my host family—which included a prominent retired physician—were less sympathetic with the teachers and believed they were representing the issues unfairly. Members of my host family felt strongly that the teachers should be in their classrooms teaching.

Thus, I was exposed regularly to viewpoints that contrasted sharply. It was challenging to honestly share my thoughts about the issues in a diplomatic way while also demonstrating sensitivity and respect for the perspectives of all. I believe that I genuinely succeeded in this important goal by consistently listening and responding as caringly as possible.

At the same time, I was reminded that social, political, and economic issues are complex and that local problems are inextricably related to conditions throughout the nation and the world. These experiences reaffirmed my strong belief that we all share a vested interest in improving opportunities for employment that can provide a living wage as well as for universal education and health care and for freedom of expression.

I would be happy to share the final Spanish-language report that I wrote about my experiences in Oaxaca with the Peace Corps selection committee, if requested. I will always cherish my memories of those weeks in Oaxaca.

## My Peace Corps Application Motivation Statement (Essay 2)

*Peace Corps service presents major physical, emotional, and intellectual challenges. You have provided information on how you qualify for Peace Corps service elsewhere in the application. In the space below, please provide a statement (between 250–500 words) that includes:*
*1) Your reasons for wanting to serve as a Peace Corps Volunteer; and*
*2) How these reasons are related to your past experiences and life goals.*

As my husband and I approach retirement, we are excited about the possibility of expanding our experiences by living and working in an international environment where we could increase our knowledge in our areas of interest while contributing to the development and well-being of others. This shared desire builds on several past experiences and life goals.

As a person of Euro-American ancestry, I have benefited from numerous cross-cultural experiences throughout my lifetime, and I am eager to explore communities in other places of the world. My husband and I are adoptive parents. We have five adult children and several grandchildren who are of Euro-American, African-American, Vietnamese-American, and Mexican-American ancestries.

Beyond homes in Michigan and California (USA), we've traveled, lived, and worked in regions of Germany, South Africa, and Mexico. I have developed conversational proficiency in German and Spanish—to a greater and lesser degree, respectively. We have valued our international experiences and have encouraged our children and grandchildren to consider similar opportunities. In essence, we want to be good role models and to exhibit for them a great joy in venturing forth in the world, taking interest in the lives of others, and contributing however we are able.

I was born in Detroit, Michigan, in 1942. My dad was a veteran of World War II, and he was a Detroit firefighter. During the postwar years, I was deeply affected by the socioeconomic conditions in this major metropolis. At this time, large numbers of African-Americans seeking employment and improved living conditions migrated from the South into segregated neighborhoods in Detroit.

As a child, I was keenly aware of the disparities between blacks and whites in housing, employment, education, and health care. So-called race riots and other forms of what people labeled as "unrest" occurred in and around the Detroit area between the early 1940s and 1970, when my husband and I relocated to Northern California (where we have lived ever since). As a firefighter, my dad often was involved in putting out fires and giving emergency medical treatment to victims of violence in the inner-city environments.

A childhood experience was powerful for me. In 1954, when I was in seventh or eighth grade, my teacher introduced a biography published by Scholastic, Inc., written by Dorothy Sterling and entitled *The Story of Harriet Tubman: Freedom Train*. My teacher was a gifted storyteller, and he typically selected children's literature that was relevant and appropriate for the young adolescents in his classes. My teacher read a chapter of this book to us at the close of each day for several weeks.

The story was spellbinding. I had never heard about the Underground Railroad before, and the narrative captured my imagination while at the same time inspiring in me a profound respect for this woman of courage and integrity. I wanted to emulate Harriet Tubman, and I developed a strong sense of appreciation for the suffering, loss, forbearance, and endurance of African Americans along with sincere feelings of compassion and kinship for these brothers and sisters.

At the same time, my teacher was not overly sentimental. He read the story to us in an honest and compelling way and highlighted the author's authentic descriptions, which portrayed each person—including Harriet Tubman—as having a mixture of both positive and negative characteristics.

Through this experience, I came to realize that all of us have flaws and that all of us, likewise, deserve to be treated with respect for our dignity and worth as human beings.

My lifelong passion for multicultural education and anti-racist curricula most certainly began at the time of these memorable experiences in Detroit.

My decision to pursue a career in education was encouraged also by the experiences I had at Wayne State University—a culturally and ethnically diverse inner-city campus—where I learned how to translate my respect for the value of students' diverse languages and cultural backgrounds into action as an educator and parent and to effectively support the success of *all* children in my classrooms, schools, and communities. A Peace Corps experience would help me continue along this path.

# *Appendix B*

## Description of Peace Corps Volunteer Service by Country Director Daniel Evans Regarding Sally Botzler

After a competitive application process stressing applicant skills, adaptability, and cross-cultural understanding, Sally Botzler and her husband Rick were invited into Peace Corps Mexico (PCM) service in November 2008 following their retirement as professors at Humboldt State University in Arcata, California. Rick and Sally Botzler entered into duty on March 3, 2009, attending Staging Events for two days in Washington, D.C.

Following her arrival in Mexico on March 4, 2009, Sally participated in an intensive 12-week pre-service training program in the City of Querétaro, Mexico. Language training included approximately 185 hours of Spanish. In addition, there were approximately 167.5 hours of sector training focusing on environmental models and practices in Mexico; and approximately 100 hours of training in Mexican culture, religion, economics, politics, and assorted health, safety, and "survival" skills. Sally lived with a Mexican host family in the City of Querétaro during the training period.

As a volunteer in the PCM Environment Program, Sally was assigned to assist the Ecological Group in the Sierra Gorda Biosphere Reserve (SGBR) located in the northern sector of the State of Querétaro. Based on the PCM Environment Program objectives, Sally's goals for volunteer service in the Biosphere Reserve were written collaboratively with her SGBR Counterpart Marina Rendón during a Counterpart Workshop at the Peace Corps Mexico offices on May 21, 2009. Marina is the Coordinator of the Virtual Campus for the Sierra Gorda Earth Center. The goals for Sally as a volunteer included familiarizing herself with SGBR strategies in sustainable development with a conservation economy, translating SGBR documents, and helping create connections between SGBR and universities.

Sally successfully completed pre-service training and was sworn in as a Volunteer on May 22, 2009. Following the Swearing-In Ceremony, Sally and her husband Rick moved on May 25, 2009, to the small town of Jalpan de Serra, Querétaro, to begin working with the Ecological Group in the Sierra Gorda Biosphere Reserve.

Sally reported directly to her supervisor, Sierra Gorda Administrative and Public Relations Coordinator Laura Pérez-Arce. During the first months of her service, Sally visited several micro-enterprises and ecotourism sites in the SGBR region. For example, she visited the Embroidery Workshop women's collaborative in La Colgada, and she spent the day with the Environmental Education team during their presentations about migratory birds of the region at a small school in the remote Sierra Gorda town of Bucareli.

Sally participated in a full week of on-site and field study activities designed to expose educators from diverse parts of the country to the distinctive SGBR approach to sustainable development.

Drawing from her background in Education, Sally prepared a report in Spanish for Marina Rendón that highlighted her observations, reflections, and recommendations. Subsequently, based on her past experience in teaching online courses, Sally also translated a set of resources about assessing the effectiveness of online education, which she gave to Marina for use with the advisors in the Virtual Campus program.

During the fall 2009 semester, Sally successfully completed the online SGBR diploma course, "Teaching and Learning for a Sustainable Future," which is based on the official UNESCO curriculum for its Decade of Education for a Sustainable Future. Sally's growing familiarity with SGBR programs and projects allowed her to ever-more accurately translate organizational documents.

As part of the diploma course requirements, each participant developed a project focused on solid waste management. Sally created a bilingual book about two "environmental visionaries": the Sierra Gorda General Director and Ashoka Fellow Pati Ruíz Corzo and the well-known U.S. activist Tim McKay who served as the Executive Director of the Northcoast Environmental Center in Northern California for over 30 years.

Toward the end of her period of PCM volunteer service, after having the Spanish sections of the bilingual text carefully edited by native speakers, Sally began working to find an agent to assist her in locating an appropriate publisher for the manuscript. Even if it is not published, Sally plans to use the bilingual material in presentations for children and youth in the Sierra Gorda of Mexico and in Northern California where she lives. Since she authored the book as a Peace Corps Mexico volunteer, any royalties will be shared between the Alliance for the Conservation of the Sierra Gorda and the Northcoast Environmental Center.

During her two years of service, Sally regularly translated numerous types of documents, including: formal proposals for project funding; periodic and final reports; descriptive materials for the website (located at www.sierragorda.net); monthly newsletters; conference materials; correspondence; notes for Facebook; subtitles for five videos (from English to Spanish); and other miscellaneous materials. Sally translated about 300 documents, including five videos.

In order to help forge SGBR and university connections, Sally and her husband Rick developed a three-week university course entitled "Sustainability in the Sierra Gorda Biosphere" focusing on the wide range of successful sustainable development strategies being implemented in the region such as reforestation, watershed restoration, carbon sequestration, holistic management, intensive (instead of extensive) cattle ranching, sanitation, environmental education, micro-enterprise and ecotourism development, and various initiatives aimed at improving the well-being of the environment and the people living within it. The course was submitted to the Humboldt State University (HSU) Extended Education Sierra Institute program and was tentatively approved to offer in July 2011.

The Chair of the HSU Department of Environmental Science and Management signed his approval of the course and it was authorized for 4 units of university credit by the Dean's Office in the College of Natural Resources and Sciences. The Chair encouraged faculty in the College to promote the course among their students; he was very impressed with the syllabus, goals, and learning activities, and suggested that the course be used to fulfill requirements in students' majors. However, in March 2011, the Chancellor of the California State University made the decision to disallow any international study programs in Mexico due to security issues in the country. At this point, Sally and Rick plan to return to the Sierra Gorda to teach the course in July 2012.

Sally also supported the Sierra Gorda in its initiative to expand international ecotourism in the region by enrolling in the online Ecotourism Certificate Program (ECP) at Humboldt State University. Beginning with the first of three courses in fall 2010, Sally focused all assignments for the courses on Sierra Gorda Ecotours destinations. She also collaborated with Sierra Gorda Ecotours Coordinator Margarita Pedraza Muñoz and her staff in developing proposed itineraries for international ecotourists. Sally worked with representatives of Road Scholar, Gap Adventures, and Mountain Travel-Sobek in an effort to market the ecotourism destinations.

In March 2011, due to his exposure to the remarkable biodiversity of the region, Michael Sweeney, Director of Humboldt State University's Ecotourism Certificate Program, and his wife Leslie accepted the invitation to come to the Sierra Gorda to take a reconnaissance trip to some of the Sierra Gorda Ecotours destinations. Following his visit, Michael sent a detailed report about his observations and impressions of the ecotourism itinerary as well as many well-received and very concrete recommendations for Sierra Gorda leaders in moving toward their goal of helping the region become a world-class destination.

In addition to her work in these areas, at the request of Sierra Gorda staff members and with the approval of General Director Pati Ruíz Corzo, Sally designed weekly English language classes for SG staff and their colleagues, which she taught from February 2010 to May 2011. She facilitated classes at basic, intermediate, and advanced levels as well as a class designed to help participants prepare to take the TOEFL exam. Over the course of the 15 months, she facilitated over 150 hour-long classes with a total of 38 participants attending among the four levels.

Additionally, as a Secondary Project, Sally and her husband Rick developed a pen pal exchange program between children enrolled in primary schools in the Sierra Gorda and children attending a Spanish-immersion elementary program at Morris School in the McKinleyville, California, community where the Botzlers live. Two of their grandchildren are among the pen pal program participants.

In her work with classes of 1st, 2nd, and 3rd graders during her two years of PCM volunteer service, Sally collaborated with four school administrators, eight classroom teachers, and over 180 children who wrote letters in Spanish to one another. Despite occasional problems with timeliness of postal system deliveries, some children exchanged five letters over the two-year period. Sally plans to continue supporting the pen pal program after she returns to California, and she has made arrangements to send and receive the packets of letters with a SGBR staff member who has a child in one of the classrooms.

Sally and Rick learned about the Eco-Club movement during their PCM service. In the Sierra Gorda, Eco-Clubs have been organized by Eco-Club Coordinator Salvador Ortiz. Eco-Clubs support the development of youth leadership in promoting all aspects of school and community environmental responsibility. At this time, there are no official Eco-Clubs in the U.S., and the Botzlers are working with Mr. Ortiz to launch an official Eco-Club in their home community. They would love to one day accompany a group of youth from Northern California to a regional

Eco-Club meeting in the Sierra Gorda and witness the first face-to-face meetings of some of the pen pals.

In June 2010, Rick and Sally hosted their children and grandchildren for a week of vacation in Mexico. For most of them, this was their first experience of traveling in Mexico, and it was a valuable learning experience. In addition, one of their sons came to the Sierra Gorda for a week at Christmastime that same year, and he, too, found the experience enjoyable and educational. Also, a graduate student from Humboldt State University visited briefly, and she expressed interest in future collaboration with the Sierra Gorda Biosphere Reserve. In all cases, Peace Corps Goals Two and Three were addressed. Rick and Sally also have cordially invited many of the Sierra Gorda and Peace Corps colleagues to visit them in California.

Throughout the two years of PCM service, Sally and Rick also routinely sent e-mail updates to family and friends in the U.S., Germany, and Japan about their experiences as Peace Corps Mexico volunteers. Over 85 people received their updates, responding very positively to the information. The Botzlers also co-hosted a Thanksgiving Day dinner on November 25, 2010, along with PCM Country Director Daniel Evans and his wife Julia Tully. The festive dinner was attended by 37 Sierra Gorda colleagues.

During her two years of volunteer service, Sally also participated in several PCM in-service events including the Mid-Service and Close-of-Service Conferences, the 3rd Annual Biodiversity Forum, and the PCM Program Evaluation Working Group meetings. At the time of her Close of Service conference, Sally was tested by a certified examiner using the Peace Corps Language Proficiency Interview (LPI). At that time, she was evaluated as being at an advanced (medium) level in her oral Spanish proficiency.

In conclusion, Sally Botzler served successfully for 2 years as a Peace Corps Mexico Volunteer. Pursuant to section 5(f) of the Peace Corps Act, 22 USC 2504(f), as amended, any former Volunteer employed by the United States Government following her Peace Corps Volunteer service is entitled to have any period of satisfactory Peace Corps service credited for purposes of retirement, seniority, reduction in force, leave, and other privileges based on length of Government service.

This is to certify in accordance with Executive Order 11103 of April 10, 1963, that Sally Botzler served successfully as a Peace Corps Volunteer. Her service ended on May 22, 2011. She is therefore eligible to be appointed as a career-conditional employee in the competitive civil service on a non-competitive basis. This benefit under the Executive Order extends for a period of one year after termination of Volunteer service, except that the employing agency may extend the period for up to three years for a former Volunteer who enters military service, pursues studies at a recognized institution of higher learning, or engages in other activities that, in the view of the appointing agency, warrant extension of the period.

Signed and dated on April 27, 2011 by:
Daniel Evans, PCM Country Director

## Description of Peace Corps Volunteer Service
## Regarding Richard G. Botzler

After a competitive application process stressing applicant skills, adaptability, and cross-cultural understanding, Richard G. (Rick) Botzler was invited into Peace Corps service. He initially was assigned to assist the Sierra Gorda Biosphere Reserve for work with wildlife of the region and for assessment of carbon sequestration among landholders of the Reserve.

Mr. Botzler entered into duty on 3 March 2009. Beginning 4 March 2009, he participated in an intensive 12-week pre-service training program in Querétaro, Mexico. Language training included approximately 185 hours of Spanish. In addition, there were approximately 167.5 hours of sector training focusing on environmental models and practices in Mexico; approximately 100 hours of training in Mexican culture, religion, economics, politics, and assorted health and safety skills; as well as a home stay with a Mexican host family to learn more about cultural practices in Mexico.

Rick successfully completed pre-service training and was sworn in as a Volunteer on 22 May 2009. He initially was assigned to the Sierra Gorda Biosphere Reserve from 23 May 2009 to 26 June 2010. In this period, Rick reported directly to Public Relations Supervisor, Laura Pérez-Arce and supported the work of the Reserve in several ways.

Initially, Rick worked with field cameras set up to monitor animal biodiversity of the region. Soon after, Rick also reviewed and completed landholder contracts for carbon sales, including calculations of the carbon production on private plots of land as well as appropriate compensation for the carbon captured and stored (carbon sequestration). He developed a file of past and current agreements signed by donors for the Sierra Gorda carbon sequestration program.

Rick also developed a survey for donors using the Sierra Gorda carbon offset program and another for those who considered using the Sierra Gorda offset program but later declined to do so.

Rick summarized several carbon footprint measures used by Sierra Gorda in relation to the carbon footprint models of World Land Trust. He also explored and organized information on many of the methods used in calculating carbon footprints as well as the types of carbon offset "packages" environmental organizations were offering to potential clients.

Rick translated and refined trail guides and informational bulletins for several Sierra Gorda ecotourism sites. He also organized and updated the library records for all books and other resource materials of the Reserve. Rick worked to establish a more direct relationship between the Sierra Gorda Biosphere Reserve (Querétaro) and that of the Sierra Gorda Biosphere Reserve (Guanajuato).

Rick edited the English grammar of numerous articles translated into English. He also completed translations from Spanish to English on videotaped narratives of participants at a July 2009 Social Entrepreneurship workshop as well as a number of reports and documents of the Reserve. He occasionally translated English letters into Spanish.

Rick began a collaborative project with Salvador (Chava) Ortiz Hernández, Director of Sierra Gorda Eco-Clubs to enhance science education among Eco-Club youth of the Sierra Gorda region. As part of this work, Rick presented a Spanish-language overview of the scientific method to a regional meeting of 65 Eco-Club leaders at the Sierra Gorda Earth Center in April 2010, illustrated with the example of a study on the prevalence and distribution of *Batrachochytrium dendrobatidis*, a fungal pathogen causing large scale population declines and extinctions of amphibians on a world-wide basis. In collaboration with his wife, Sally, Rick continues to work with Mr. Ortiz in the effort to launch an Eco-Club in northern California—perhaps the first in the U.S.

Rick collaborated with his wife, Sally Botzler (also a PCM Volunteer in the Sierra Gorda Biosphere Reserve), to establish a pen pal exchange program between 1st, 2nd, and 4th grade students in the elementary school in their home town (McKinleyville) in northern California and those respective grades in the Benito Juárez and Melchor Ocampo primary schools in Jalpan de Serra, Mexico. Rick worked in the Benito Juárez School with a class of 4th graders, and then with the same class of 5th graders the following year; fifty-three 4th and 5th grade students participated in his portion of the pen pal exchange.

During this first year, Rick also collaborated with his wife, Sally, and the Sierra Gorda Ecotours staff in designing an English-language program itinerary focused on the unique features and strategies of major ecotourism sites in the Sierra Gorda region. The course was intended to be offered through Road Scholar (formerly Exploritas and, also, formerly Elderhostel); however, Road Scholar chose not to include the itinerary due to declining interest of their clientele for trips to Mexico in light of news media reports about safety and security issues in the country.

Following discussions with the Reserve leaders and with his Peace Corps Mexico program manager, Rick shifted from his work at the Reserve and assumed new volunteer responsibilities within the broader Sierra Gorda region. In collaboration with Professor Ángel García, School Director and sole teacher at the Vicente Guerrero Elementary School in the small, rural community of San Vicente (250 inhabitants) within the County of Jalpan de Serra, Rick served as a volunteer teacher each Wednesday in a class of 21 first- through third-grade students (mornings) and a class of 19 fourth- through sixth-grade students (afternoons). Rick's responsibilities included teaching English, biology, ecology, and general science. In collaboration with Sierra Gorda Biosphere Reserve staff, Rick also assisted the students and community to reestablish a recycling program, begin an organic garden, host two environmental education program presentations, and receive two solar ovens for use in their school cafeteria.

In Cuatro Palos, a community of 200 inhabitants (40 families) within the adjacent County of Pinal de Amoles, Rick established a training program for five 8-13 year-old guides to help them develop in working with international tourists visiting their area. The training sessions included key information about the history, ecology, and biology of the region as well as information about the distinctive features of Cuatro Palos. The young guides gained skill in accompanying tourists on hikes and became more confident about giving presentations. Two of the guides accompanied Michael Sweeney, Director of the Ecotourism Certificate Program at Humboldt State University during his reconnaissance trip to the region; Michael subsequently prepared an assessment of the training program, which Rick used to make improvements.

In light of increasing numbers of international tourists anticipated in the region, Rick also provided English-language classes for the Cuatro Palos guides as well as for seven other community members and staff in the Office of Tourism in Pinal de Amoles.

Rick also offered four English "Circle of Discussion" classes to a total of 90 students over each of two trimesters at the Universidad Tecnológica de San Juan del Río (UTSJR), Jalpan Academic Unit—two classes for Ecotourism students and two for Business Development students. Rick also assisted two UTSJR faculty members in the process of preparing research proposals for their doctoral studies. In addition, Rick presented a workshop on writing for scientific publication to 25 members of the Science and Engineering faculty at the main UTSJR campus, San Juan del Río, on 25 February 2011.

Rick collaborated with Professor Gabriela Parra Olea, Universidad Nacional Autónoma de Mexico (UNAM) in a research study to evaluate the presence and distribution of *Batrachochytrium dendrobatidis*, a serious pathogenic chytrid fungus, among amphibians of the Sierra Gorda region. They expect to present their findings at the Wildlife Disease Association Annual Conference, Quebec City, Canada, in August 2011.

Additionally, Rick collaborated with his wife, Sally, to design a three-week course on sustainable development with a conservation economy through Humboldt State University's (HSU) Sierra Institute in its Extended Education program. The course was strongly supported at HSU, but ultimately the California State University Chancellor's office cancelled all international programs for Mexico in 2011 because of safety concerns.

Rick served as a scientific reviewer for the journal, ACTA TROPICA, for a submitted manuscript dealing with variations in human blood values in relation to the parasite burdens of the people. The study was based on research in a rural community in Brazil. Rick also participated as an expert in wildlife diseases for a doctoral thesis survey by a Michigan State University student in January to December 2010. The study was entitled "Human Dimensions of Wildlife Management Research."

The recently developed bilateral agreement between the United States and Mexico (2011) is designed to expand the opportunities for cooperative work between Peace Corps Mexico and the country of Mexico in areas beyond the traditional work with the National Council of Science and Technology (Consejo Nacional de Ciencia y Tecnología: CONACYT) and the Secretary for Environment and Natural Resources (Secretaría de Medio Ambiente y Recursos Naturales: SEMARNAT). In the activities during his second year, Rick participated in several areas of non-traditional Peace Corps volunteer service that may anticipate some of these new directions. Hopefully, these non-traditional volunteer activities provide administrators both in Peace Corps Mexico and in Mexican agencies some useful opportunities to explore and evaluate possibilities for future collaboration.

During his two years of PCM volunteer service, Rick also participated in several scientific meetings in Mexico. A Peace Corps Mexico–sponsored Biodiversity Conference was held 16 to 20 August 2009 in Querétaro. The Primer Congreso en Ecología de Enfermedades y Medicina de la Conservación (KALAANKAB) was held in Puerto de Veracruz, Veracruz, 4 to 6 November 2009. The Encuentro Nacional sobre Biodiversidad, Conservación y Restauración Ecológica en México 2009, occurred in Morelia, Michoacán, 17 to 19 November 2009. The third Biodiversity Conference sponsored by Peace Corps Mexico was held in Amealco, 29 March to 1 April 2011. In addition, Rick made several professional presentations during his work as a Peace Corps Mexico Volunteer, both at some of these meetings and in response to other invitations.

Botzler, R. G. 2009. "*Batrachochytrium dendrobatidis*: Un riesgo potencialmente grave para los anfibios de México," presented in Spanish at the Primer Congreso en Ecología de Enfermedades y Medicina de la Conservación KALAANKAB, Puerto de Veracruz, Veracruz, 4 to 6 November 2009.

Botzler, R. G. 2009. "Avian cholera in Northern California," presented in English at the Primer Congreso en Ecología de Enfermedades y Medicina de la Conservación KALAANKAB, Puerto de Veracruz, Veracruz, 4 to 6 November 2009.

Botzler, R. G. 2009. "Perspectivas éticas y su relación con programas de conservación de la biodiversidad," presented in Spanish at the Encuentro Nacional sobre Biodiversidad, Conservación y Restauración Ecológica en México 2009, Morelia, Michoacán, 17 to 19 November 2009.

Botzler, R. G. 2010. "El método de ciencia y el hongo en anfibios," an invited presentation to a regional meeting of Eco-Club leaders in Jalpan de Serra. Presented in Spanish, 16 April 2010.

Botzler, R. G. 2011. "Redacción de artículos científicos y éticas de ciencia," an invited presentation in Spanish to the Faculty of Science and Engineering, Universidad Tecnológica de San Juan del Río. (25 February 2011).

Botzler, S. J. & Botzler, R.G. (2011). "Teaching English as a Second Language," an invited presentation in English to Peace Corps Mexico Volunteers in the PCM 09 Environment Program. Amealco, Mexico, 31 March 2011.

Rick also wrote an article for Peace Corps volunteers and staff assessing current attitudes and policies toward use of basic scientific research among Natural Protected Areas of Mexico, with recommendations for stronger research programs. The English-language version was presented in *La Piñata* No. 9 (January 2011), and is entitled, "Basic Scientific Research in Mexico's Natural Protected Areas: A Proposal." The Spanish-language version is entitled, "Investigación Científica Básica en Áreas Naturales Protegidas de México: Una propuesta."

Mr. Botzler served successfully for 24 months as a Peace Corps Mexico Volunteer. At the completion of service, Rick was tested by a Peace Corps Language Proficiency Interview (LPI) certified examiner. At that time he was evaluated at "intermediate-medium" in oral Spanish proficiency.

Pursuant to section 5(f) of the Peace Corps Act, 22 USC 2504(f), as amended, any former Volunteer employed by the United States Government following his Peace Corps Volunteer service is entitled to have any period of satisfactory Peace Corps service credited for purposes of retirement, seniority, reduction in force, leave, and other privileges based on length of Government service.

This is to certify, in accordance with Executive Order 11103 of April 10, 1963, that Richard G. Botzler served successfully as a Peace Corps Volunteer. His service ended on 22 May 2011. He therefore is eligible to be appointed as a career-conditional employee in the competitive civil service on a non-competitive basis. This benefit under the Executive Order extends for a period of one year after termination of Volunteer service, except that the employing agency may extend the period for up to three years for a former Volunteer who enters military service, pursues studies at a recognized institution of higher learning, or engages in other activities that, in the view of the appointing agency, warrant extension of the period.

Signed and dated on April 27, 2011 by:
Daniel Evans, PCM Country Director

# *Acknowledgments*

Rick and I are grateful to the individuals listed here and to many, many others who provided personal and professional support and assistance to us as volunteers in Peace Corps Mexico and during the Ecoclub development.

### At Humboldt State University

Megan McDrew, HSU Peace Corps recruiter; HSU friends Sue
Lee and Archie Mossman; and many HSU colleagues
Ward Angles, HSU extended education coordinator, and staff
Michael Sweeney, director, Ecotourism Certificate Program

### At Peace Corps Mexico, Querétaro

Byron Battle, PCM country director, and Margarita Battle, PCM support provider
Ángel Piñeda, PCM environment program manager
Benita Luna and Beatriz Charles, PCM environment program coordinators
Lourdes Gonzalez-Alarcon and Cynthia Galaz, PCM medical
officers, and Malena Vázquez, PCM security officer
Regina Montaño, PCM program director; Adriana Niembro,
resource coordinator; and Rosa Elena Jiménez, cashier
Anna Toness and Joshua Spetter, PCM training coordinators; Rodrigo
Lopez, administrator; and Armando Reyna, general assistant.
Daniel Evans, PCM country director; Julia Tully, PCM support
provider; and the other PCM staff and volunteers

### Sierra Gorda Ecological Group

Martha (Pati) Ruíz Corzo, director, and Roberto Pedraza, codirector
Víctor Manuel Idelfonso Apolinar, codirector, and Roberto Pedraza Ruíz, program coordinator
Margarita Pedraza Muñoz, ecotours coordinator
Laura Pérez-Arce, executive secretary, and Óscar Estrada, accountant

### National and International Ecoclub Promotors and Consultants in El Paso, Texas

Sylvia Sillas and Edmundo Rodríguez, national Ecoclub promoters
Anne Doherty-Stephan, administrator, El Chamizal National
Park; and Gustavo Iturralde, PAHO consultant

## Bilingual McKinleyville Ecoclub and Project Consultants

Michael Davies-Hughes, superintendent, McKinleyville Union School District
Jeff Brock, MUSD business manager, and many other MUSD staff
Jane Carlton, Ecoclub facilitator, McKinleyville Middle School
Susan López, facilitator, Morris School
Consultants: Byrd Lochtie, Marissa O'Neill, and Debbie González
Clark Davis, elk project leader
Rick Botzler, amphibian project leader
Stan Schmidt, garden project leader
Stacy Beck and Rees Hughes, trail stewards project leaders
Keith Bensen, fish and wildlife biologist, Redwood National Park Ticket-to-Ride Project
McKinleyville Community Services District staff
Joyce King and others, McKinleyville Land Trust board
McKinleyville Union School District families, teachers, administrators, and staff

## Amphibian Research Project Consultants

Drs. Mourad Gabriel and Greta Wengert; Dr. Janet Foley; Dr. Karen Pope; and Don Ashton

## Ecoclub Leadership Team

Marisol Madriz, Spanish-language liaison and project participant
Jane Carlton and Susan López, Ecoclub facilitators
Sarah Botzler, ELT advisor and project participant
Katie Cutshall, Ecoclub parent fundraising and Ticket to Ride
Clark and Danielle Davis, advisors/workshop leaders and participants
Kendra Anderson and Amanda Reed, Ecoclub parent advisors
Julia Davis and Xenia Sánchez-Madriz, Youth Ecoclub participants
Elizabeth Rivera, Ecoclub teacher advisor and chaperone

## Youth Project Leaders

Anastasi Rivera, president
Areli Toscano, president
Hannia Sánchez-Madriz, vice president
Nate Botzler, vice president
Ashlyn Reed, treasurer
Dakota Spirit-Anderson, project leader
Adriana Cutshall, project leader
Yulian Gutierrez, project leader

And many more relatives, friends, Ecoclub youth, and participating families!

Printed in the United States
By Bookmasters